Competitive Supply Chains

Competitive Supply Chains

A Value-Based Management Perspective

Enver Yücesan
Professor of Operations Management, INSEAD, France

First published 2007 by
PALGRAVE MACMILLAN
Houndmills, Basingstoke, Hampshire RG21 6XS and
175 Fifth Avenue, New York, N. Y. 10010
Companies and representatives throughout the world

PALGRAVE MACMILLAN is the global academic imprint of the
Palgrave Macmillan division of St. Martin's Press, LLC and of
Palgrave Macmillan Ltd. Macmillan® is a registered trademark in the
United States, United Kingdom and other countries. Palgrave is a
registered trademark in the European Union and other countries.

ISBN-13: 978-0-230-51567-3   hardback
ISBN-10: 0-230-51567-3   hardback

This book is printed on paper suitable for recycling and made from
fully managed and sustained forest sources. Logging, pulping and
manufacturing processes are expected to conform to the environmental
regulations of the country of origin.

A catalogue record for this book is available from the British Library.

A catalog record for this book is available from the Library of Congress.

10   9   8   7   6   5   4   3   2   1
16   15 14 13 12 11 10 09 08 07

Printed and bound in Great Britain by
Antony Rowe Ltd, Chippenham and Eastbourne

To the loving memory of my dear mother,
Dr. Mürüvvet Aydın Yücesan.

Table of Contents

List of Figures

List of Tables

Preface

It is generally accepted that Supply Chain Management (SCM) started gathering steam in early 1990s when a Kurt Salmon and Associates study concluded that the demand-supply mismatches were costing the U.S. grocery industry $30 billion a year.[1] Up until then, SCM was considered to be an obscure back office activity, typically labelled as "warehousing and distribution" or, a bit more gloriously, "logistics." A ruthless wake-up call, $30 billion represents a shocking number when one realizes that low-margin products such as toothpaste, broccoli, and flour are at stake in this industry. Moreover, in this setting, keeping additional stock to provide high levels of customer service is risky due to enormous variety in products and their short shelf life. On the other hand, stock-outs, which are typically around 7% of sales for better managed companies, lead to lost sales, not only for the grocery store, but ultimately for the overall industry, including the retailer *and* the manufacturer, as the customer abandons the purchase altogether. It was quickly discovered that other industries were also facing similar challenges. Under such difficult circumstances, many industries have undertaken revolutionary initiatives in streamlining their go-to-market strategies. Over the past decade, a flurry of research, development, and deployment has transformed SCM into a mature discipline in its own right.

Within that period, numerous books and thousands of articles have appeared on the topic contributing to the rapid advancement of the field. However, two gaps in the literature still persist. First, activities within the realm of SCM are typically viewed as cost centers whereby cost minimization remains the key focus of most SCM streamlining efforts. To compound the problem, the divide between the performance metrics typically used in the trenches (such as inventory turns, order fulfilment rates, order turnaround times) and the financial indicators typically monitored by the upper management and the investors (such as economic profit [EP], Return On Capital Employed [ROCE], Return On Net Assets [RONA]) remains wide. This book adopts a value-based management (VBM) perspective, in which SCM is deployed for both value creation and value capture. SCM solutions are developed and deployed to create value for everyone who comes into contact with a company's products and services. In this setting, "value" could be created by simply minimizing costs. On the other hand, there are situations in which cost minimization simply destroys value for the stakeholders, necessitating alternative strategies. VBM therefore enables the adoption of a wider business perspective for SCM. Furthermore, such a perspective also allows us to map operational performance metrics to the financial performance indicators in a straightforward fashion, enabling the evaluation of whether or not the proposed supply chain solutions are ultimately value enhancing or value destroying.

While necessary, value creation, however, is not sufficient for value capture. There are many examples in which an innovative design introduced by one company has been successfully commercialized by another one, leaving the original inventor with little profits. This, in turn, brings us to the second gap in the literature based on the old adage that "competition is no longer between companies but between supply chains." Implicit in this statement is the assumption that modern supply chains operate as a single well-coordinated entity, like a basketball team, with a clearly defined command-and-control structure. This might have been true in the early 20th century where many industries exhibited full vertical integration. Today's supply chains, however, are ecosystems, with no clear governance – or command-and-control – structure, consisting of independent organizations. As these "economically rational agents" interact with each other, there might be serious misalignments within the ecosystem due to diverging local priorities, which might hinder the performance of the overall supply chain. In other words, having a star player in each position does not necessarily guarantee victory as a team. The performance of the Dream Team representing the United States at the 2006 World Basketball Championships in Japan is a relevant benchmark for modern SCM. In many industries ranging from personal computers to airlines, different supply chain members display widely different profitability levels. This book, therefore, adopts a decentralized view of the supply chain and puts an emphasis on economic mechanisms to promote coordination and collaboration within this ecosystem, so that the value created by the supply chain is captured in an equitable fashion by all its members. In other words, we would like not only our basketball team to win, but also to make sure that all the players are recognized – and remunerated – for their contribution to the team effort.

Finally, it is important to realize that the supply chain solution, which achieves the desired targets in value creation and value capture, is necessarily temporary. As products have expiration dates, as processes become obsolete, supply chain solutions also have limited shelf lives. Changes in competitive forces, in customer preferences, in technology, and even in legislature may render the existing supply chain solution inadequate. One must therefore keep an eye on these key drivers and not hesitate to go back to the drawing board when the existing supply chain solution can no longer support the changing business strategy.

Another novelty embodied in this book is the framework through which the material is presented. This framework is summarized in Figure 0.1. The horizontal axis represents the scope of the book. It starts with a vision: VBM, the challenge of providing value to everyone who comes in contact with a company's products and services. This vision is operationalized through a strategy formulation, which defines the company's business model, its affinity for product and process innovation, and its investment in developing and acquiring resources. The strategy is then deployed through key processes that are at the heart of SCM. These processes represent the concrete

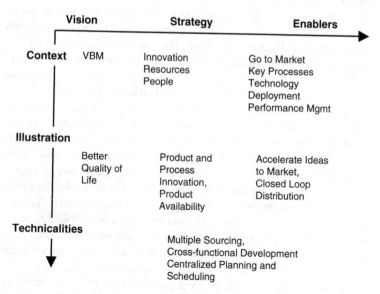

Figure 0.1 Value-based SCM framework for *Coloplast*.

enablers of VBM. The focus is then on deployment with an explicit discussion of the technologies, structures, and skills required for the rollout of effective supply chain solutions. The adoption of such a broad scope has a dual purpose. First, we wish to draw the attention of top managers to the strategic role of SCM in value creation and capture, and put SCM on the CEO's agenda. Conversely, we would like to broaden the perspective of supply chain professionals by demonstrating explicitly the contributions they make to the firm's overall strategy through the initiatives they undertake in designing, coordinating, and managing supply chains.

The vertical axis represents the scale of the book. It starts with the motivation by establishing the context of the problem to be addressed. An illustration in the form of a mini case study is then provided to render the discussion concrete. It is worth emphasizing that these illustrations will not come from frequently cited (and often abused) examples, but from companies such as *Coloplast, CIBA Vision, PSA, PPR, Firmenich, Nissan,* and *Mattel,* all best-in-class examples deserving broader exposure. Finally, we present not only alternative solutions to the problem at hand, but also provide the technical details that constitute the basis of the proposed solution. Such an approach guarantees both the relevance of the topics addressed in this book and the rigor underlying the proposed supply chain solution. We have, however, paid particular attention so that the technical developments throughout the text do not distract attention from the main discussion. Hence, the reader can enter into the technicalities only when he/she feels necessary to do so.

Figure 0.1 also provides an illustration from *Coloplast,* a Danish wound care company, whose vision is to be the preferred source of medical devices and associated services contributing to a better quality of life. *Coloplast* operationalizes this vision through innovation, both in products (which provide improved functionality, hence higher comfort levels, to patients) and in processes (which develop not only efficient manufacturing capabilities, but also an agile supply chain for quick deliveries). To this end, processes have been put in place to accelerate new product development and market introduction as well as to have a balanced product distribution on a global scale. All of these processes are based on sound materials management principles.

After an introductory chapter that establish the necessary working definitions, Chapter 2 offers a concise definition of "value" from a financial perspective. Operational drivers of "value" are then identified with the objective of determining those SCM initiatives that contribute to the value-creation challenge of an organization. Chapter 3 then focuses on value creation by concurrently emphasizing the product, process, and supply chain design. In particular, we emphasize the temporary nature of a competitive advantage and the resulting necessity of continuously developing new supply chain solutions in the face of a continuously evolving competitive landscape. Many value-creating initiatives, however, entail a cost-service trade-off. To assess the magnitude of this trade-off, Chapter 4 introduces a materials management model. This model can be deployed not only to guide the positioning of a company's goods or services in the short run, but also to assess the impact of investments in new product, process and supply chain design in the long run.

Chapter 5 focuses on value capture. In particular, it describes both short-term and long-term initiatives to encourage collaboration in a decentralized supply chain. SCM is an information intensive discipline. Chapter 6 therefore summarizes the impact of Information Technology (IT) on SCM practices; it also highlights the enhancing role of emerging web-based technologies in SCM. Just like products, services are also conceived, produced and delivered through supply chains. There are nevertheless significant differences between product and service supply chains. These differences are discussed in Chapter 7 along with guidelines of coordinating the two types of ecosystems. Chapter 8 offers some concluding comments.

A television advertisement for *UPS* at the height of the dot-com boom clearly showed the importance of effective supply chain strategies. The advertisement starts with a group of young entrepreneurs sitting in front of a computer terminal and counting down for the launch of their new Web-based business. Once they go live, they start waiting for customer orders. The first customer order, signalled with a "bing" on their computer, is greeted with a wild cheer by all the entrepreneurs. The cheers grow wilder as the second, the fifth, the tenth, and the fiftieth orders trickle in. However, as the trickling soon turns into a shower of orders that cross the threshold of the thousandth customer order, their cheer quickly turns into deep anxiety: how are they going to deliver all these orders? This book therefore adopts the perspective that SCM should be viewed as the effective deployment of value-based business strategies.

Acknowledgments

The idea for this book first came from Xavier de Montgros, who has been undertaking impressive global supply chain initiatives for personal computers at the Desktop Division of *Hewlett-Packard* (*HP*). While we were having heated discussions both in Grenoble and in Fontainebleau regarding the scope of the book and the depth of exposition, Xavier was asked to assume wider responsibilities within *HP*, making it impossible for him to dedicate any further time and effort to our "book project." Once bit, however, I could not abandon the project even after losing my coauthor. Over the two years that followed Xavier's departure, I wrote and rewrote many of the chapters, reformulated parts of the exposition, and expanded the scope of the discussion. In this endeavor, I have fully benefited from the advantages of working at a leading business school. First, two of my great colleagues and friends at INSEAD, David Young and Kevin Kaiser, shaped my thinking about supply chain management by giving me a clear perspective on value-based management. I also had the opportunity to interact with hundreds of supply chain professionals from Asia, Europe, and the Americas, who either attended my courses at INSEAD or who had generously collaborated with me on various breakthrough supply chain projects. They are simply too numerous to mention by name in this limited space. I am grateful to all of them for providing me with a valuable reality check. Finally, colleagues in my home department of Technology and Operations Management have been a constant source of intellectual stimulation.

Writing a book is like having a baby: it takes as much time as you have. I therefore owe a big thank-you to my wife, Jae, and to my children, Elliot and Justine, for their understanding over the time I spent with the manuscript rather than with them. I am also very grateful to my editors at Palgrave Macmillan, who made the publication process a smooth one for me.

1
Introduction

1. Motivation

Supply Chain Management (SCM) plays a significant role in value creation on a global scale. Figure 1.1 illustrates the growth of global manufacturing and global trade as one of the principal drivers of worldwide wealth creation. Based on sustained foreign direct investment (FDI), as shown in Figure 1.2, it would be safe to conclude that this growth is bound to continue, as companies rush to take advantage of not only lower labor costs (Figure 1.3), but also emerging centers of excellence such as China and India. In supporting such sustained economic activity, supply chain costs in developed economies are estimated to be around 10% of the GDP, surpassing, for example, $1 trillion in the United States in 2001. In developing countries, on the other hand, supply chain costs may represent up to 30% of GDP. This is due to both the lower-value products and services produced by these economies and the higher transaction costs engendered by poorer infrastructure in communication and transportation. Supply chain costs typically consist of

- 58% for transportation
- 30% for inventory carrying
- 8% for warehousing
- 4% for logistics administration

In fast-moving consumer goods, a fiercely competitive industry, price erosion over a decade has been quite dramatic, as illustrated by

1

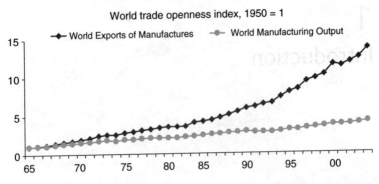

Figure 1.1 Progress in world output and exports of manufactured products.

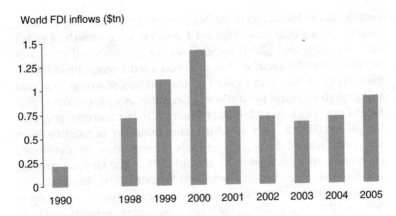

Figure 1.2 The evolution of FDI.

Figure 1.4. Similarly, the average selling price of a personal computer (PC) has been decreasing by 10–15% per year over the past decade. In the automotive industry, a 5% price reduction is not even negotiated between a manufacturer and its suppliers. With margins rapidly shrinking, there is growing pressure on supply chain managers to minimize procurement, production, and distribution costs. Such a focus on cost reduction in SCM has been typical in many industries facing global competition.

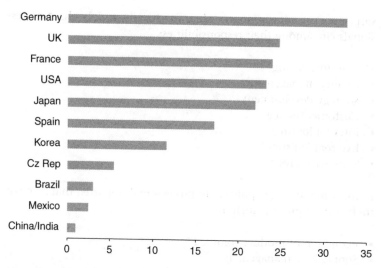

Figure 1.3 Hourly compensation for production workers in manufacturing ($, including benefits).

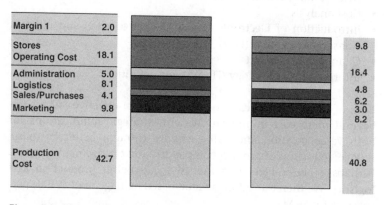

Figure 1.4 The cost structure in *FMCG* (1985–95).

While one cannot (and should not) ignore costs, in this book, we have chosen to emphasize the enabling role of supply chains in *value creation* and *value capture*. In fact, a recent survey of supply chain managers in France by the weekly *L'Usine Nouvelle* has revealed that the responsibilities of these professionals have a scope that largely surpasses cost minimization.[1] More specifically, supply chain professionals cite among their responsibilities:

- Sales forecasting
- Quality management
- Strategy development
- Customer service
- Internal logistics
- External logistics
- Systems analysis

In the same survey, supply chain professionals reported that some of their current projects include

- Reduction of product complexity
- Supply base management
- Agile manufacturing
- Production planning
- Distribution network design
- Cost analysis
- Introduction of Electronic Data Interchange (EDI) and Efficient Consumer Response (ECR)
- Change management
- Information Technology (IT) Systems definition

Both of these lists indicate that the impact of effective SCM is felt beyond mere cost minimization, with strategic ramifications for both value creation and value capture through better customer service, reduction of product complexity, and change management. Perhaps a better P&L does indeed mean better production and logistics. We therefore adopt a value-based management (VBM) perspective for SCM.

2. Working definitions

To discuss the role a supply chain plays in value creation and capture, we first need to define these terms. Scholars in strategy and economics equate "value" with the customer's *willingness to pay* (WTP), which reflects the benefits perceived by the customer. As illustrated by the

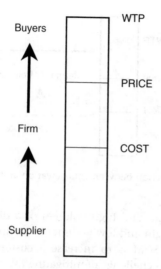

Figure 1.5 Defining value as WTP.

"value stick" in Figure 1.5, WTP is the maximum amount that a customer would pay for a firm's products or services; it is typically different from price. The value created by a transaction is then equal to the difference between its cost and the customer's WTP. The former includes both procurement costs and internal conversion costs. This definition implicitly captures the fact that a firm can only create value by operating together with its suppliers and customers.

As stated above, the difference between WTP and cost is equal to the value *created* in a supply chain. While the difference between price and cost determines the margin earned by the firm, the difference between WTP and price (the value *captured* by the customer or the consumer surplus, as economists would refer to it) drives the sales volume. The product of margin and volume thus yields the profit, the value *captured* by the firm. Figure 1.6 then reflects an interesting trade-off. Value created by a firm is an upper bound on the value it can capture. If the firm sets a higher price (increasing its margin), it may drive down the volume of sales. Alternatively, if the firm lowers its price (reducing its margin), it may increase its sales volume, achieving the same level of profitability. This is why management scholars[2] advocate that a firm might adopt either a cost leadership

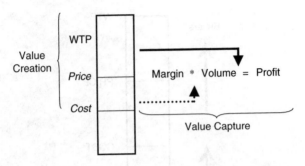

Figure 1.6   The interaction between value creation and value capture.

position (low margin and high volume) or a differentiator (niche) position (high margin and low volume) to be profitable. One of the key challenges in SCM is to increase a customer's WTP without increasing cost. This challenge of mitigating the cost-service trade-off is the main topic of Chapter 4.

Now that we have a conceptual definition of "value" that will be further refined and operationalized in Chapter 2, we turn to the definition of a supply chain. A supply chain is a *network* consisting of suppliers, manufacturers, distributors, retailers, and customers (Figure 1.7). The network supports three types of flows that require careful planning and close coordination:

(i) *material flows*, which represent physical product flows from suppliers to customers as well as the reverse flows for product returns, servicing, remanufacturing, and recycling;

(ii) *information flows*, which represent order transmission and order tracking, coordinating the physical flows; and

(iii) *financial flows*, which represent credit terms, payment schedules, and consignment arrangements.

Note that all three flows are bi-directional. Traditionally, one used to think that goods and services would go from suppliers downstream through a series of value-adding steps all the way to the final customer. Particularly for manufactured products, manufacturers are increasingly accountable for taking back their product at the end of the product's life cycle and disposing of it in an environmentally responsible

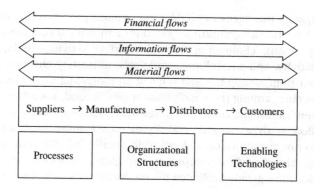

Figure 1.7 Another perspective on the supply chain.

fashion.[3] We therefore talk about bi-directional or *closed-loop* supply chains. Similarly, information was thought to flow exclusively from the market to all the tiers upstream in a supply chain. Innovative organizations like *UPS* or *Dell* have shown the value of providing the customer with real-time information about the status of their package or their order, respectively. Finally, financial flows are no longer simply based on 60-day payment terms. Facilities ranging from consignment stocks to various risk-sharing arrangements have also made financial flows bi-directional.

The supply chain, a *platform* to coordinate these three flows, is supported by three pillars:

(i) *processes*, which encompass such value-adding activities as logistics, new product development, order fulfillment, and after-sales service;

(ii) *organizational structures*, which encompass not only a range of relationships from total vertical integration to networked companies, but also performance measurement and incentive schemes to make such relationships sustainable; and

(iii) *enabling technologies*, which encompass both process and information technologies.

The above definition hides some important subtleties. First and foremost, modern SCM has deeply benefited from a series of improvement initiatives. Over the past few decades, the waves of just-in-time (JIT), total quality management (TQM), and business process reengineering (BPR) have had a significant impact on the individual components of supply chains, eliminating non-value-adding activities, enhancing productivity, and streamlining workflows, ultimately enabling us to step out from among the four walls of an individual site to focus on the *interfaces* among these individual stages. Second, the advances in communication and computation technologies have made it possible to collect, analyze, transmit, and deploy huge amounts of data necessary to run operations on a global scale. Finally, infrastructure investments, along with developments in global transportation and logistics, have greatly facilitated the movement of goods (Figure 1.1).

One big challenge, however, remains. Industry structures, which used to be dominated by vertically integrated organizations, have largely been replaced by networked organizations or loosely coupled ecosystems. In the absence of a clear command and control structure, coordination among the members of a supply chain is not trivial, necessitating the implementation of explicit incentive schemes for aligning the divergent and often conflicting economic interests of its members. In other words, while the challenge of value creation is shared by the members of an ecosystem, value capture remains a contentious issue.

Supply chains perform two principal functions: the *physical* function of transformation, storage, and transportation, and the *market mediation* function of matching demand and supply in a highly volatile, uncertain environment. While the physical function has been extensively studied within the Production Control and Inventory Management literature,[4] innovative approaches to the market mediation function have recently been emerging. These approaches, which are classified in Figure 1.8, will be the focus of this book.

The key reason for our focus on *market mediation* is the drastic consequences of a potential demand-supply mismatch. In 1996, a retail study by the Voluntary Interindustry Commerce Standards (VICS) Association found that stock-outs occurred at an average rate of 8.2%, corresponding to 6.5% of all retail sales.[5] For a retailer, part of this stock-out situation (3.4% of the 6.5%) was offset by alternative sales at the store, while the remainder (3.1% of the 6.5%) represented a lost sale. For manufacturers, the implications were even worse: out of the 6.5% of stock-outs, only 1.5% was recouped in alternative purchases from the same manufacturer.

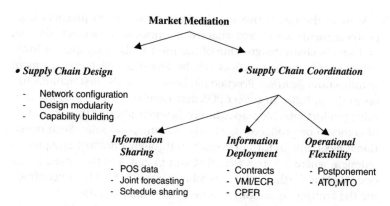

Figure 1.8 Matching demand and supply in a supply chain.

On the other hand, holding inventory provides limited relief in spite of its high price tag. According to the U.S. Department of Commerce, retail sales in the U.S. reached $3.2 trillion in 2000. To support this volume of sales, it was estimated that retailers held approximately $372 billion in inventory. Wholesalers held an additional $307 billion to supply the retailers, while the combined tiers of manufacturers held about $472 billion in inventory. Thus, it was estimated that total inventory across the value chain added up to around $1.1 trillion.

Market mediation has two key enablers. *Supply chain coordination* is concerned with the coordination of the three types of flows over the network. Effective coordination strategies combine a range of approaches for enhancing supply chain transparency through information sharing (e.g., sharing point-of-sales [POS] data with the manufacturer) and information deployment (e.g., vendor-managed inventories [VMI], ECR, and collaborative planning, forecasting and replenishment [CPFR] initiatives) as well as for operational flexibility (e.g., assemble-to-order [ATO] and make-to-order [MTO] systems) to be able to react to timely information. These approaches may facilitate new forms of organizational structures (e.g., process orientation) and new forms of inter-organizational collaboration (e.g., outsourcing via third-party service providers). Information and communication technologies facilitating closer collaboration and promoting supply chain transparency are crucial for effective coordination. Innovative product and process designs are a prerequisite for operational flexibility.

Most of the innovative supply chain coordination practices (e.g., postponement) are indeed enabled by innovative product, process, and supply chain design. One of the most visible examples of innovative supply chain practices can be found at the Italian garment manufacturer *Benetton*. *Benetton* has been one of the first manufacturers in the industry to collect POS data from key retail stores to determine product mix. More specifically, *Benetton* adjusted the assortment of colors to be produced by closely tracking retail sales. Such operational flexibility, in turn, was enabled through a product and process redesign, where sweaters were first knit in gray and then dyed to the desired color. Further volume flexibility was achieved by subcontracting the knitting operations to a network of small textile labs.

Supply chain design, therefore, is concerned not only with the configuration of a network, namely, the specification of customer zones, selection of manufacturing and distribution facilities, and allocation of product families to these sites, but also with the prioritization of the capabilities to be developed and retained internally, and the forging of new partnerships with other entities along a supply network. According to Fine,[6] supply chain design ought to be thought of as "the capability to design and assemble assets, organizations, skill sets, and competencies for a *series* of competitive advantages, rather than a set of activities held together by low transaction costs." This dynamic view is necessary in a fast-evolving world where new products and emerging distribution channels necessitate a continuous review of supply chain design decisions. Just as product design has an enormous impact on manufacturing performance, superior supply chain design offers significant payoffs in supply chain coordination.

In the next chapter, we will first introduce the VBM framework that will help us not only to operationalize the concept of value but also to derive performance metrics and cascade them throughout the supply chain. We will then establish how the market mediation function of supply chains can help in value creation and value capture through design and coordination, respectively. In particular, we will discuss supply chain design for value creation, while the focus of supply chain coordination will be on value capture.

2
Value-Based Management: The Guiding Principle for SCM

1. The role of SCM

VBM is playing an increasingly significant role in shaping corporate strategies. Since the key mission of SCM is to develop and deploy effective solutions to enable the deployment and execution of corporate strategies, SCM should also adopt a VBM perspective. VBM-based SCM has therefore two intertwined dimensions, as depicted in Figure 2.1. On the one hand, VBM should enable *value creation* through product and/or process innovation, both of which should drive a customer's WTP. While product innovation may enable the deployment of niche strategies, process innovation may lead to cost leadership. In both cases, however, innovation plays a key role in differentiating a firm from its competitors or in avoiding the commoditization of its products and services.

While value creation by a firm is necessary, it does not automatically ensure value capture by the same firm. For example, the Internet has undeniably created tremendous value for the business world. Researchers conceiving this global network, however, did certainly not capture this value. Similarly, air travel provides a significant amount of value for business and leisure travelers. While aircraft manufacturers or airport operators may capture the lion's share of value along with business travelers, airline companies are trying very hard to simply survive. There are plenty of other examples where an innovation introduced by one firm has been turned into a runaway commercial success by another one. VBM-based SCM should therefore

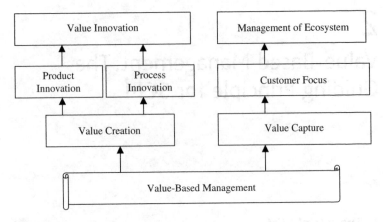

Figure 2.1   SCM as an enabler of VBM.

also focus on *value capture* through a more effective management of the relationships with the partners within the firm's ecosystem.

As we will discuss in greater detail in Chapter 3, value creation starts with three-dimensional concurrent engineering (3D-CE): the simultaneous design of the product, of the process, and of the supply chain.[1] Product design decisions are concerned with the adoption of an adequate architecture, ranging from a fully modular to totally integrated designs. Process design, on the other hand, is concerned with the selection of resources that are either dedicated (favoring economies of scale) or flexible (favoring economies of scope). Finally, supply chain design not only considers the configuration of the supply network, but also focuses on the key make-or-buy (outsourcing vs insourcing) decisions.

Value capture, on the other hand, focuses on the coordination of the firms within the supply chain. This is an inherently difficult task as vertically integrated industries with clear command-and-control structures have been replaced by network structures where each echelon is owned and operated by an independent (and economically rational) firm. Alignment of independent players in such decentralized ecosystems is the main challenge in supply chain coordination, including the design and implementation of collaborative practices. In other words, incentives should be designed to enable value capture by a firm that is commensurate with the value it adds to the ecosystem.

While we have identified value creation and value capture as the two principal dimensions of SCM, we have only defined "value" within the context of the "value stick." For supply chain design and coordination, however, such a concept has to be operationalized in a way that maps the operational metrics under the daily control of a supply chain professional to the financial metrics monitored by higher levels of management. We will provide such a definition in the next section.

2. Operationalizing the definition of value

Businesses should have one paramount goal: the creation of shareholder value. Such a bold statement may, at first, appear to reflect a cold view of the world as seen from the Wall Street. Some might argue that customers should always come first. Without customer satisfaction, a company may not survive. Others may advocate that without dedicated employees, it is not even possible to bring goods and services to markets. What about the suppliers? The community? The environment? In fact, in its 1995 annual report, *Coca Cola* states that it "provides value to everyone who touches it." Whether it is customers who enjoy the soft drinks, employees who work in a stimulating environment, bottlers who enjoy attractive profit margins, or shareholders who are wealthier because of the company's strong financial performance, everyone is supposedly better off. How can one simultaneously satisfy all these stakeholders? Ultimately, one can delight customers by providing goods and services for free. One can make the employees happy through attractive pay packages and extremely flexible working conditions. Similarly, generous payment terms would always be welcome by the suppliers or the channel members. Sponsorship of local activities is deeply appreciated by local communities. These demands are diverging and often conflicting requirements on a company's limited resources.

Yet, there needs to be a balanced approach to providing value. The concept of *shareholder value* provides this necessary balance. Shareholder value is not at all about shareholders; it is simply a measure that strives to establish a balance among all stakeholders. Let us first define concisely what we mean by "value" before discussing whose value we are talking about. Consider the calculation of the *free cash flow* (or the residual cash flow) for a company:

Revenues
- − Cost of Goods Sold (COGS)
- − Selling, general, and administrative (SG&A) expenses
- − Depreciation
- = Earnings before interest and tax (EBIT) − Taxes on EBIT
= Net operating profit after tax (NOPAT)
- + Depreciation
- − Increase in working capital
- − Capital expenditures
= **Free cash flow**

This calculation shows that once the company has satisfied its customers and therefore generated revenues, it has to compensate its employees and pay its suppliers. Depreciation is not a cash flow, but a tax shield; we therefore subtract it first from the revenues to calculate the tax base. The company must then comply with its tax obligations. This gives us Net operating profit after tax (NOPAT) or Net profit from operations. As depreciation is simply a tax shield, it is added back to calculate the free cash flow after allowing for potential increases in the working capital and for other capital investments. This free cash flow is what enables the firm to return some cash to its shareholders in the form of dividends or share buybacks.

Note that shareholders come *last* in this calculation, staking a claim to what is left on the table: free (or residual) cash flow. While there is a legal obligation towards employees, suppliers, channel partners, and creditors, there is no such contract with the shareholders. The latter invest in your company with the belief in your managerial capabilities and, thanks to them, the expectation of earning higher returns than in other investment opportunities. Hence, as the *residual* claim, only shareholder value can reflect how well all of the complex relationships within the ecosystem of a firm are managed simultaneously. Put another way, shareholder value is the only measure whose calculation requires *complete* information. By focusing on shareholder value, one can be sure to properly manage the diverse and often conflicting interests of the other stakeholders of the firm. From a technical perspective, maximizing shareholder value is equivalent to the maximization of the residual cash flow in an optimization setting, which would automatically strike a balance among its individual components. By managing for shareholder value, *Coca Cola* does indeed satisfy all of its key stakeholders, namely its customers, its employees, its suppliers, and, of course, its shareholders.

We can then define "value" as the present value of all the future free cash flows generated by a company discounted at the company's cost of capital. This is indeed the gauge market analysts use in evaluating publicly traded firms. Value-driven businesses have also adopted this model in capital investment appraisal (i.e., supply chain design) and performance measurement (i.e., incentive design for supply chain coordination).

While the maximization of shareholder value, the paramount goal of a firm, is intrinsically able to align the requirements of the various constituencies of a firm, we still need to operationalize this concept. In particular, we need a performance metric that would monitor, encourage, and reward value creation. Finance professionals have been proposing various such metrics. We will, however, focus on an intuitive one: *economic profit* (EP).[2] For a company to create value, it is necessary for that company to cover not only its operating expenses, but also its capital charges. In other words, a company has to generate EP, which is defined as:

Net sales
- − Operating expenses
- = Operating profit (EBIT)
- − Taxes on EBIT
- = NOPAT − Capital charges (Invested capital * WACC)
- **= EP or EVA®**

where WACC is the weighted average cost of capital for the firm. EP, also referred to as EVA (economic value added), forms the basis of VBM.

Note that EP is different from accounting profit. Accountants focus on Net income (=EBIT − Interest − Tax), where interest expense is based on a firm's debt. On the other hand, EP (EP = EBIT − Taxes − Capital charges = NOPAT − Capital charges) takes into consideration *all* capital employed in running the business. In that sense, it measures the effectiveness with which companies manage all the resources (human, intellectual, material, and financial) invested in them.

As it is defined, however, EP may not necessarily be within the *line of sight* of a supply chain professional. In other words, in her day-to-day decision making responsibilities, a supply chain manager may not necessarily have a direct impact on EP. A supply chain manager should therefore focus on both strategic and operational *drivers* that directly influence EP. To this end, first note that, as EP = NOPAT – Capital charges, where NOPAT is reflected within the Profit and Loss (P&L) Statement, whereas the capital charges are found in the balance sheet. Let us then consider a balance sheet in further detail:

Assets	Liabilities & Owners' Equity
Cash	Short-term debt
Receivables	Short-term NIBL
Inventory	Long-term debt
Prepayments	Other long-term liabilities
Fixed assets	Shareholder equity

The balance sheet reflects what a firm owns (assets) and what it owes (liabilities), typically starting with the most liquid items (e.g., cash) and ending with least liquid ones (e.g., fixed assets). In other words, liabilities show the source of financing for the assets. We will convert this traditional balance sheet into a *managerial balance sheet* by netting the nonfinancial accounts labeled Short-term NIBL (noninterest bearing liabilities) against short-term operating assets (receivables + inventories + prepayments). The left hand side of this managerial balance sheet is referred to as "invested capital;" "capital employed" appears on the right hand side. This yields:

Invested Capital	Capital Employed
Cash	Short-term debt
Working Capital Requirement	Long-term debt
	Other long-term liabilities
Fixed assets	Shareholder equity

Net assets (or capital employed) are investments for which the firm's capital providers expect, and managers – including supply chain managers – must deliver, a competitive return. For a supply chain manager, fixed assets typically represent strategic supply chain design decisions typically associated with network configuration.

Recall that as long as the return generated from the use of "net" assets (the sum of cash, working capital requirement [WCR], and fixed assets) exceeds the cost of invested capital, EP is positive. We calculate the return on net assets (RONA) – or the return on capital employed (ROCE) – as follows:

$$RONA = NOPAT/(\text{Net assets}) \Leftrightarrow ROCE = NOPAT/(\text{Capital employed})$$

Since EP = [(ROCE – WACC) * Invested capital], it is positive when ROCE is greater than WACC, and negative when ROCE is less than WACC. This relationship immediately suggests a value-creating rule of thumb for the supply chain manager: invest only in value-creating projects, namely in those with a positive net present value (NPV), where NPV is the present value of all future free cash flows generated by the project and discounted at the firm's WACC.

From an operational perspective, however, it is necessary to break these high-level financial metrics into their operational drivers and cascade them throughout the organization. Figure 2.2 illustrates such a cascading exercise. ROCE, taken as a level-1 performance metric, can be written as the ratio of NOPAT and capital employed. By multiplying and dividing this ratio by sales, we obtain two key drivers of ROCE as level-2 metrics: operating margin (= NOPAT/Sales) and capital turnover (= Sales/Capital employed). One can then continue

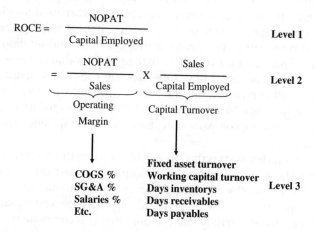

Figure 2.2   Cascading EP across the organizational levels.

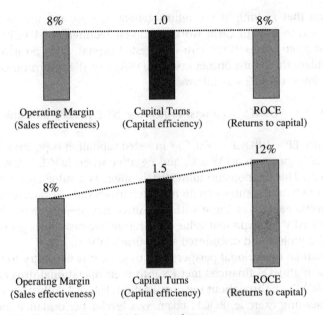

Figure 2.3 Creating value by higher capital turns.

this cascading exercise by identifying the key drivers of operating margin (e.g., COGS, SG&A, etc.) and of capital turnover (e.g., Working capital turnover, Days of inventory, Days of receivables, etc.).

Figure 2.3 shows the critical role of capital turnover in generating superior returns on capital employed. Such an exercise must also be done for a supply chain professional by first identifying the key value drivers within her sphere of responsibility and by designing adequate performance measures that promote value-creating decisions. Figure 2.4 shows how some leading companies invest their capital. *Dell* compares quite favorably with both *IBM* and *HP* in terms of not only Net Fixed Assets (NFA), but also for its negative WCR. As a trading company, this chart also shows the effective SCM at *Li & Fung*.

To get another perspective on ROCE, let us revisit our managerial balance sheet and consider the column of invested capital (or net assets). A supply chain manager does not (and should not) manage cash. This is the task of Corporate Treasury. A supply chain manager, however, should carefully manage the other two components of net assets, namely the WCR and the fixed assets.

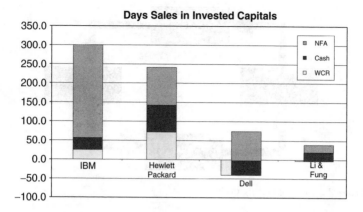

Figure 2.4 Deploying the invested capital.

While the fixed assets are impacted by the supply chain design decisions, WCR is directly concerned with supply chain coordination. To see the importance of managing WCR, consider the *operating cycle* of a firm, sometimes referred to as the cash-to-cash cycle, as illustrated in Figure 2.5.

For a typical manufacturing company, the operating cycle starts when the firm purchases materials, parts, and components. These materials are then transformed into finished products. We refer to the time it takes from the acquisition of input materials to the production of finished goods as the *manufacturing period*. The products are then sold, which typically requires a *sales period*, which may include warehousing, transportation, and delivery. Since the product remains within the company as inventory until it is sold, the sum of the manufacturing period and sales period equals the *inventory period*. Customers, however, do not pay for the product immediately after delivery. The length of time for the firm to collect cash from customers after a sale has taken place is called the *receivables period*.

Within such an operating cycle, a firm must therefore invest in inventory and receivables. Moreover, the firm might have prepaid expenses such as the rental of extra warehouse space as well as operating cash for day-to-day operations. The total investment necessary in an operating cycle therefore includes:

Inventories + Receivables + Prepaid expenses and other current assets + Operating cash

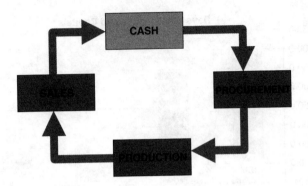

Figure 2.5 The operating cycle.

The firm, however, is not the only entity that invests into an operating cycle. Suppliers, employees, customers, and even the government contribute. WCR is therefore defined as the "net" investment a firm has to make in an operating cycle, namely:

WCR = (Inventories + Receivables + Other Current Assets + Operating cash) – (Accounts payable + Accrued expenses + Advances from customers)

Accounts payable include the money you owe to your suppliers, representing their investment into your operating cycle. Accrued expenses include salaries that are only paid at the end of the month – hence, the employees' contribution – and the taxes that will be paid at their due date – hence, the government's contribution to your operating cycle. If customers also prepay for their purchases, that money also reduces WCR for the firm.

To emphasize the importance of effective WCR management, consider Table 2.1. *REL Consultancy* (now the *Hackett Group*) estimates that, if the top 1000 European corporations manage their WCR – i.e., their relations with the customers and suppliers as well as their stocks – more efficiently, they may be able to generate 580 billion euros of cash. In fact, between 2001 and 2003, these corporations were able to reduce their WCR by 9%, which enabled a 6% reduction in their net debt.

The EP perspective therefore compels supply chain managers (in fact, all managers) to generate competitive returns on WCR, just as it does for cash and fixed assets. Table 2.2 summarizes the operational

Table 2.1 WCR for 1000 large European corporations

Country	No. of days for customer payments	Δ in one year	Stocks	Δ in one year	No. of days for paying suppliers	Δ in one year	WCR	Δ in one year
B	47.1	−1.4	40.1	−5.4	43.7	2.3	43.4	−8.2
DK	49.0	−2.4	39.1	8.7	30.2	−0.1	57.8	3.5
F	68.6	0.4	35.5	−5.2	59.7	1.9	44.4	−6.0
– auto	60.0	−106	34.7	−6.2	59.0	1.9	35.6	−11
D	73.1	1.6	38.2	−0.7	33.3	2.6	78.0	0.1
–auto	46.4	−3.5	36.7	−2.8	33.9	2.0	49.2	−6.5
I	94.4	−3.7	43.2	6.9	69.0	−3.1	68.6	2.1
–auto	78.8	−5.8	40.6	5.9	63.6	−3.9	55.8	−0.1
NL	42.5	−0.9	27.2	1.0	32.5	−0.7	37.2	0.3
N	49.0	−4.2	22.1	−8.6	32.9	2.6	38.2	−12
SE	64.8	5.7	27.0	−1.2	68.3	9.1	23.5	−9.7
SW	67.3	−0.3	37.0	−1.8	33.1	0	71.1	−1.2
–auto	55.8	−1.6	34.1	−1.2	31.5	−1.9	58.4	−1.2
CH	60.5	2.6	49.3	−0.6	29.6	6.7	74.2	−0.8
UK	40.5	−0.4	30.9	−5.5	32.8	−0.6	38.5	−4.4
Total Europe	59.9	−0.4	35.1	−2.6	41.7	1.1	53.3	−3.0
–auto	59.1	−1.9	34.2	−3.4	41.3	0.9	43.9	−5.5

Source: REL Consultancy Group (Le Figaro, 19 September 2004)

Table 2.2   Operational Drivers of EP

Drivers of EP	Operational Initiatives
Increase ROCE	Cut costs
	Improve working capital efficiency
	Cut throughput times
	Take pricing initiatives
	Better scrutinize capital investment
	proposals
Decrease WACC	Use debt optimally
	Buyback shares
	Promote transparency
Increase Invested Capital	Undertake positive NPV investments
	Adopt profitable growth strategies
Decrease Invested Capital	Sell assets that are worth more to others
	Restructure unprofitable businesses
Extend the competitive advantage period through	Product innovation
	Process innovation
	Brand equity
	Intellectual capital

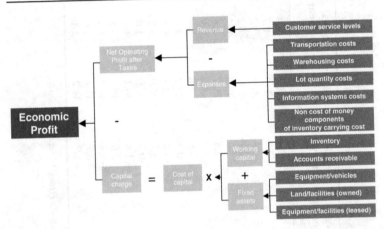

Figure 2.6   EP in SCM.

drivers that create EP, while Figure 2.6 depicts those EP drivers that are within a supply chain manager's line of sight are. From a strategic perspective, the supply chain manager should be responsible for customer service levels, which, in turn, are driven by product, process, and supply chain design choices. The choices made in configuring the supply chain will have a direct impact on fixed assets. The product and process design choices, in turn, will become constraints on operational drivers that will impact both expenses and WCR.

In other words, Figure 2.6 depicts the operational drivers of EP, which promotes the generation of cash from operations that cover not only the operating expenses, but also the financing charges. NOPAT can be enhanced by increasing revenues and reducing expenses; the operational drivers here typically represent strategic decisions on customer service as well as innovative product, process, and supply chain design initiatives to contain cost-to-serve. The capital charges, on the other hand, can be contained through effective working capital and fixed asset management; the operational drivers here represent tactical initiatives such as materials management, management of receivables and payables, and effective use of capacity.

3. Summary

It should come as no surprise that the share price of the *European Aeronautic Defense and Space Company (EADS)*, the parent of *Airbus*, sunk by 26% in a single day after *Airbus* announced delays of up to two years in delivering the company's newest jumbo jet, the A380. Such a delay caused by complications related to the wiring of A380 would limit deliveries to just seven airplanes in 2007 rather than 25, as was originally planned, pushing the breakeven point for the entire project beyond 2010. *EADS* further disclosed that the *Airbus* delays were likely to reduce the parent company's operating profit by around 500 million euros per year between 2007 and 2010.[3] Ultimately, A380 delays led to an executive shake-up at the company with the resignations of the co-CEO of *EADS* and the CEO of *Airbus*.[4] In fact, in a large-scale study of 519 supply chain glitches announced by publicly held organizations between 1989 and 2000, Hendricks and Singhal found that the public announcement of an operational mishap led to an abnormal decrease of 10.3% in shareholder value.[5]

In short, recent empirical work has established a clear causal relationship between operational drivers and shareholder value. Supported by such strong empirical evidence, the linkage between a company's supply chain performance and its shareholder value is succinctly captured by the EP framework. In this chapter, we have therefore focused on the following key points:

- "Shareholder value" is a framework to balance the (often divergent and conflicting) requirements of the stakeholders in a firm's ecosystem.
- EVA (or EP) is an effective metric to monitor and promote the creation of shareholder value.
- EVA (or EP) represents a "line of sight" problem for supply chain managers.
- Supply chain managers should therefore focus on the operational drivers of EVA to design a lean and agile supply chain.

3

Value Creation: Dynamic Supply Chain Design

1. Motivation

Xerox spent most of the 1980s painfully regaining, inch by inch, the market share it had lost so dramatically to new entrants and reestablishing the dominant position it had occupied in the market in the 1970s. In Europe, for instance, *Xerox*'s market share tumbled from 18% in early 1980s to 4% in 1986, stabilizing at around 15% in 1989. Central to this comeback was an obsessive dedication to quality and the introduction of JIT manufacturing and distribution. In fact, *Xerox* spent the second half of 1980s implementing the JIT philosophy in its European manufacturing operations. In this process, *Xerox* rationalized its supply base, reducing it from 5000 suppliers to 300, enabled direct delivery into the production lines, and closed down all of its national warehouses, centralizing the distribution activities through a European Logistics Center in Holland.[1] As emphasized in Figure 3.1, this supply chain rationalization effort was accompanied by a reclassification of the product offerings, ranging from built-to-order high-end products to make-to-stock (MTS) low-end products.

While *Xerox* has been redesigning its supply chain over a five-year period, a quiet technological revolution was changing the landscape in the copier industry with digital copiers replacing analog ones. This transformation had deep implications on *Xerox*'s supply chain solution: first, the core of its supply base has shifted towards suppliers of electronic components. Second, with the changing product characteristics, a different distribution channel was emerging. Finally, as

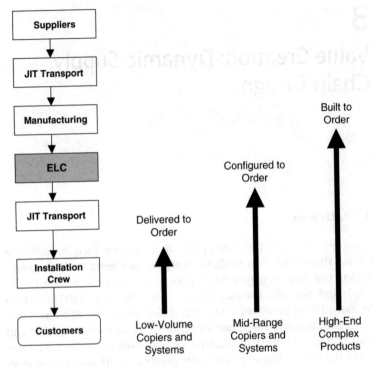

Figure 3.1   Xerox's European distribution network in 1990s.

the digital copier was integrated into the local area network in an office, the customer was no longer a maintenance, repair, and operations (MRO) procurement officer, but the information technology (IT) specialist. In short, a new supply chain solution had become necessary.

Book publishing is another industry that has experienced a similar transformation – though at a slower pace of change or *clockspeed*. Arguably, book publishing was initially an MTO business, a king or a queen commissioning the writing of *the* book. An artist with excellent calligraphy skills would then complete and deliver the manuscript. A technological breakthrough, the invention of the printing press, along with the higher tolerance levels of the Renaissance, has led to the creation of an MTS industry spanning authors, publishing houses, printers, distributors, and corner book stores. Mega bookstores reinforced the MTS practices. Another technological breakthrough, e-commerce powered by the Internet, has drastically altered the architecture of the print supply chain, rendering the retail outlet less significant. With the recent initiatives in hardware, if e-books ever fulfill their promise and become popular, on-demand publishing will turn this industry into an MTO business once again.

Another colossal industry transformation is depicted in Figures 3.2 and 3.3, which are taken from the book by Andrew Grove, *Intel's* cofounder and ex-chairman.[2] Figure 3.2 depicts the vertically integrated industry structure and the integral product architecture in the computer industry from 1975 to 1985. This period was indeed the era of not only the mainframe computers manufactured by *IBM, DEC, Burroughs, Univac, NEC* among others, but also of the closed and proprietary architectures. In this environment, if a customer purchased an operating system from a particular manufacturer, he was obliged to procure all the hardware and software from the same manufacturer as interoperability was nonexistent among these manufacturers. In other words, once you chose your camp, you were obliged to stay with it throughout the entire portfolio with no mix-and-match capability. The birth of the PC, however, has drastically modified this industry structure. *IBM*, which defined the industry inspite of its late entry, made two strategic choices. In 1980, it outsourced the manufacturing of the microprocessor to a young

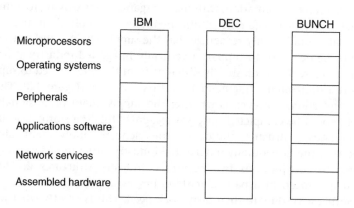

Figure 3.2 Vertical industry structure and integral product architecture in the computer industry, 1975–1985.

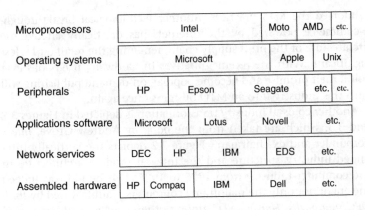

Microprocessors	Intel	Moto	AMD	etc.
Operating systems	Microsoft	Apple	Unix	
Peripherals	HP	Epson	Seagate	etc. · etc.
Applications software	Microsoft · Lotus	Novell	etc.	
Network services	DEC · HP · IBM	EDS	etc.	
Assembled hardware	HP · Compaq · IBM	Dell	etc.	

Figure 3.3 Vertical industry structure and integral product architecture in the computer industry, 1985–1995.

organization, *Intel*, and the writing of the operating system to another start-up, *Microsoft*. Moreover, to facilitate coordination within these outsourced relationships, *IBM* deviated from its tradition of closed and proprietary architectures by adopting an open and modular product architecture for the PC.

As illustrated in Figure 3.3, these economically rational decisions had drastically altered the landscape in the computer industry over the subsequent decade: full vertical integration has been replaced by horizontal fragmentation, with many organizations striving to dominate individual segments within the industry. Supply chain professionals would readily recognize that the supply chain solution that must be deployed to support a vertically integrated industry structure (Figure 3.2) is drastically different from the one needed to support a horizontally fragmented industry structure (Figure 3.3). The key question, however, is whether the supply chain professional's job would be completed once we recognize this transformation in the industry structure and deploy the adequate supply chain solution for the horizontally fragmented industry structure. As we have seen in the previous two examples, industry structures do not remain frozen in a particular state, but evolve from one state to another according to their own clockspeed. This is exactly what we have been observing in the computer industry as well. Consider, for instance, the path taken by *Intel*. After establishing its dominance in the segment for microprocessors, *Intel* has widened its footprint not only by incorporating computation and graphics capabilities into its own products, but also by influencing the decisions of hardware designers and application developers on their product lines. Similarly, after dominating the operating system segment, *Microsoft* has forayed into various other segments ranging from databases to web browsers, from enterprise applications to office productivity tools. One may think that the industry is swinging back to its original vertically integrated structure with an integral product architecture – with a different set of players.

This is indeed the thesis of Fine with his "double helix" model, illustrated in Figure 3.4,[3] whereby various forces are driving the evolution of industry structure, rendering the existing supply chain solutions inadequate.

Consider, for example, *IBM* in the mid-1970s, whose products were designed following a closed and proprietary architecture within a vertically integrated industry. On the one hand, to maintain its leading position, *IBM* had to be at the forefront in all its offerings. On the other hand, due to its own organizational rigidities and high-dimensional complexity, the company was slow in responding to

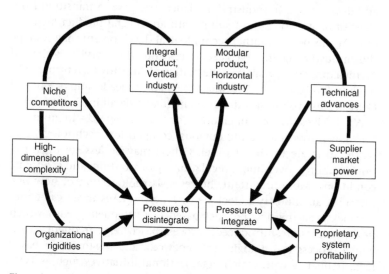

Figure 3.4 Fine's double helix model of industry evolution.

challenges by niche players, both increasing the pressure to disintegrate. Once the industry has crossed the threshold and swung to the other side of the double helix to become modular, horizontal, and fragmented, a fierce battle followed for the domination of each segment. Once a dominant player emerged in a particular segment, that player typically started exerting its influence in shaping other segments, as illustrated by *Intel* and *Microsoft* examples. This, in turn, built further pressure to integrate – perhaps around a different set of players.

The Enterprise Resource Planning (ERP) industry provides another example of the double helix. Once the client-server architecture became the accepted standard of computing, this industry's ecosystem was based on a modular product and horizontally fragmented industry structure. Application vendors such as *SAP* and *Oracle* focused on the transactional backbone, while specialty applications such as scheduling, SCM, and Customer Relationship Management (CRM) have been addressed by specialists such as *i2 Technologies*, *Manugistics*, and *Siebel* (now part of *Oracle*), respectively. Implementation was left to consultancies. This *cohabitation*, however, did not last long. As application vendors grew stronger, their footprints expanded from the transactional backbone into the areas of specialty applications and deployment. In industry's parlance, there was a transition from "best of breed" to "best of suite" with an integral product architecture. At this point, another technological development may reshape the industry again: Web Services and the Service Oriented Architecture (SOA) may provide sufficient impetus to return to the modular/horizontal setting under the platform leadership of *SAP* and *Oracle*. (This evolution is discussed in greater detail in Chapter 6.)

What drives the pace of change – or the clockspeed – in an industry? Some drivers are quite obvious: competition, technology, and power structure in the channel. Others may be less so: organizational culture, government regulations, globalization, and economic conditions. More important, however, is the question of how one measures an industry's clockspeed. Fine proposes three categories of clockspeed metrics: product based (e.g., frequency with which new products are introduced), process based (e.g., frequency with which process technologies get renewed), and organization based (e.g., frequency with which organizational initiatives such as TQM

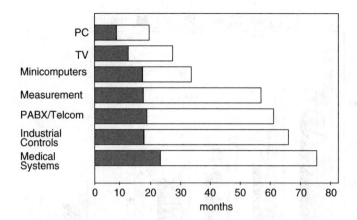

Figure 3.5 The rhythm of development activity in the electronics industry (Mendelson and Pillai, 1999).

and six-sigma are launched). From that perspective, brewing would be considered a slow clockspeed industry (on average, a new brewing process every 200 years), while airframe manufacturing for passenger aircraft would be a medium clockspeed industry (on average, one new plane program every decade), PCs and cell phones would be a fast clockspeed industry (on average, a new product every six to nine months). While this is not a concise measurement scheme, an empirical study[4] within the electronics industry provides strategic support to the argument. Figure 3.5 shows the average time in months between product redesigns, while the shaded areas represent the average duration of development projects in this industry in early 1990s. Based on this product-based clockspeed metric, one can then classify the PC industry as a high-clockspeed industry with an average of 24 months for new product introductions (with an average of 12 months of development cycle). Medical systems, on the other hand, have a slower clockspeed with a new product introduced on average every 76 months (with a development cycle of 24 weeks). The same study shows that product life cycles are indeed getting shorter. Figure 3.6 illustrates the life cycle compression over 1988–95 in all the segments of this industry.

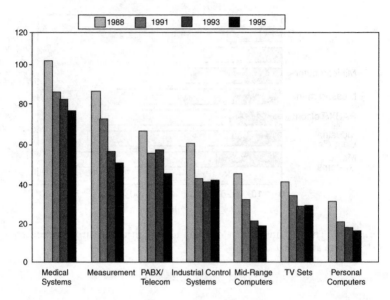

Figure 3.6   Product life cycle compression, 1988–1995 (Mendelson and Pillai, 1999).

2. The impact on supply chain design: 3D-CE

As a result of these industry dynamics, the discomforting news for the supply chain professional is that just like products and processes, supply chain solutions also have a limited shelf life. Driven by their clockspeed, industries are in constant evolution, ultimately rendering existing supply chain designs obsolete. Supply chain professionals should therefore watch their industry clockspeed closely and be ready to generate alternative solutions as industry structures evolve. In other words, they should view supply chain design as a *dynamic* process, and particularly as "the capability to design and assemble assets, organizations, skill sets, and competencies for a *series* of competitive advantages, rather than a set of activities held together by low transaction costs."

The 3D-CE is a framework for dynamic supply chain design. As illustrated in Figure 3.7, 3D-CE encourages the concurrent design of products, processes, and supply chains and explicitly considers the interfaces among these three dimensions. The objective is to render the transition from the current – but inadequate – supply chain

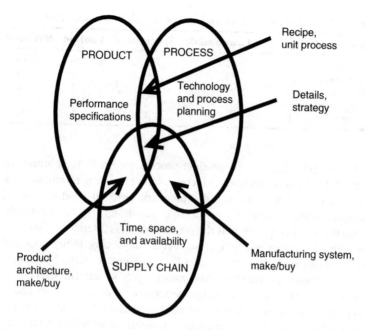

Figure 3.7 3D-CE (Fine, 1998).

solution to the next supply chain design as smooth and painless as possible by taking the decisions on product, process, and supply chain design simultaneously. Let us now consider the key interfaces to see how 3D-CE aims to achieve a smoother transition.

Concurrent product and process design is now a well-accepted idea, with a vast design-for-X literature, where X could stand for manufacturability, assembly, disassembly, or localization. *Intel's* development of successive generations of microprocessors (386, 486, Pentium, etc.) along with evolving photolithography technology (1 micron, 0.8 micron, 0.6 micron, etc.) is a classic example of concurrent product and process design. *Intel* has launched its new product, the 386 processor, on a proven 1-micron process technology. Once all the product glitches have been resolved, the next generation of the 386 processor was then launched on a new 0.8-micron process technology. Once the process technology was mastered, it was used as a basis to launch the new product, the 486 microprocessor. In this fashion, *Intel* was able to dynamically coordinate the improvements in both the product and the process designs.

Table 3.1   Product offerings of leading mountain-bike manufacturers

Characteristics	Cannondale	Specialized	VooDoo	National
End Items	110	134	1726	6240
Frame Geometry	12	6	2	3
Materials	1	6	3	2
Components per Frame	2	1.4	48	6
Colors per Model	1.25	1.25	1	104

A low-tech example of product-process interface is captured in Table 3.1, which shows the product portfolio of leading mountain-bike manufacturers.[5] If these manufacturers compete on product variety, *National* should have a considerable advantage over *Cannondale*. However, the key question at the product-process interface is how this breadth of product portfolio is achieved. *National* certainly does not have the different frame geometries that *Cannondale* offers. Nor does it have the variety in materials. *National* achieves variety through colors per model. From a process design perspective, this reliance on colors necessitates a relatively low investment in a scheduling algorithm for the painting process. For *Cannondale*, however, process design requires quick changeovers and consistently high quality welding for all frame geometries. In addition, if bicycles are offered in different materials such as steel, aluminum, and carbon fibers, separate processes need to be developed; as one cannot weld carbon, an injection moulding process must be developed. This simple example thus illustrates the importance of making product and process decisions simultaneously.

The process–supply chain interface has recently been highlighted through the market mediation role of supply chains.[6] Following Fisher's classification, a "functional product" with a stable demand pattern but thin margins would necessitate a cost-efficient supply chain, while an "innovative product" with a highly volatile demand pattern, but attractive margins, would require a responsive supply chain. Fast-moving consumer goods are a good example of functional products. For a bar of soap, a tube of toothpaste or a razor, consumers' WTP is typically driven by availability at stable prices. A bar of soap with moisturizing cream, a tube of toothpaste with tartar control, and a disposable razor with four blades, however, can be classified as innovative products. Similarly, fashion products, such as ski parkas or designer eyewear, are examples of innovative products. There is much uncertainty about customer acceptance and their

WTP; however, if the product is a success, there are significant margins to be made. While cost reduction is the overriding concern in the former family of products, agility is vital for the latter. Key characteristics of these products are summarized in Table 3.2, while key channel characteristics are listed in Table 3.3.

While the product–supply chain interface is well understood in a *static* sense, mismatches creep up as markets evolve. Consider, for example, a manufacturer selling a commoditized product through a physically efficient supply chain. Suppose that the manufacturer no longer wishes to compete on cost and decides to seek ways for differentiating its product offering by incorporating several innovative features. While he hopes to afford higher margins through this repositioning, he is also faced with increased uncertainty associated with the market's reaction to the new offering. In other words, the manufacturer has just transformed his product from a functional one into an innovative one. What we typically observe in practice is that such a product transformation is rarely accompanied by a transformation in the supply chain. Frequently, companies try to push innovative

Table 3.2 Characteristics of functional vs innovative products

Product Characteristics	Functional Product	Innovative Product
Demand	Predictable	Variable
Life Cycle	> 2 years	¼–1 year
Margin	5–20%	20–60%
Variety	Low	High
Forecast Error	10%	40–100%
Stock-out Rate	1–2%	10–40%
Average Markdown	0%	10–25%

Table 3.3 Supply chain characteristics

Channel Characteristics	Physically Efficient	Market Responsive
Purpose	Lowest cost	Agility
Manufacturing Focus	High utilization	Excess capacity
Inventory Strategy	High turns	Stock deployment
Lead Time Focus	Shorten as long as cost does not increase	Invest to reduce lead time
Product Design	Max performance at minimum cost	Modular design

products through supply chains designed for physical efficiency, incurring huge losses due to demand-supply mismatches.

The process–supply chain interface is concerned with outsourcing decisions. While such decisions are mostly based on an economic make-vs-buy analysis, one typically ignores their long-term ramifications. Outsourcing the production of an item typically entails the loss of the associated design and manufacturing capabilities. While the positive financial impact of buying an item at a cheaper rate than in-house manufacturing is felt immediately, the strategic trap, namely the loss of technological edge and manufacturing capability associated with that item, is only revealed at a much later stage when the firm tries to launch the next generation of the product only to find out that it no longer possesses some of the critical capabilities it needs in-house.

In fact, Van Weele (2005) states that "outsourcing means that the company divests itself of the resources to fulfill a particular activity to another company to focus more effectively on its own competence. The difference with subcontracting is the divestment of assets, infrastructure, people, and competencies."

To avoid such a trap, one should determine whether outsourcing decisions are driven by a shortage of manufacturing capacity or manufacturing capability. For example, it may be rational for a toy manufacturer to outsource the production of figurines associated with a movie that is currently breaking all records at the box office, while a machine tool manufacturer may wish to keep the production of a component in-house in order not to lose its own tight-tolerance machining capability even if cheaper external alternatives exist.

Outsourcing risks became evident in 2001 with the crash of the electronics market.[7] *Electronics Manufacturing Services (EMS)* had experienced stellar growth in late 1990's with massive outsourcing of production by traditional cell phone manufacturers such as *Motorola, Ericsson, Nokia,* and *Siemens* to *EMS* giants such as *Solectron, SCI Sanmina,* and *Flextronics.* Given that, with shelf lives of around six months, cell phones represented a high clockspeed industry, such outsourcing decisions were quite reasonable. The hiccup occurred when the original equipment manufacturers (OEM) thought that the forecasted downturn in this market would only affect their competitors with a limited impact on their own sales. OEMs had therefore told their contract manufacturers (CM) to continue buying the necessary components and manufacturing cell phones. When the market bottomed out in 2001 for *all* OEMs, there was $7 billion worth of inventory in that supply chain, corresponding to six months' worth of sales. Such a surplus led to a long and unpleasant discussion on finding a solution to this demand-supply mismatch. CMs argued that with a clearer picture of the marketplace due to their close relationship with the final customer, OEMs should have anticipated the downturn in the market and told them to slow down the procurement and production. OEMs, on the other hand, argued that the CMs should be in a better position to use the electronics components in stock given that CMs had a diversified customer base across the electronics industry ranging from PCs to medical devices. In an industry where inventory does not age gracefully, each party had to write off a sizeable chunk of the supply chain inventories. Ülkü et al. (2006)[8] identify conditions under which an OEM with better market information or a CM with better pooling capabilities should indeed bear the demand-supply mismatch risk.

In addition to such coordination risks due to the lack of clear governance structures, there are also long-term strategic risks. Access to latest technology is arguably at the top of the list of such strategic risks. Imagine, for example, the inability of *Intel* to introduce a new Pentium processor on the 0.13 micron technology, as *ASML* is slow in investing in the next generation of wafer steppers with higher photolithography capabilities. Similarly, imagine the inability of automobile manufacturers to launch a hybrid car because investment in hydrogen refueling stations is lagging behind. There is no point in building Ferraris if there are no highways on which to drive them. Such technology risks are analyzed by Ülkü et al. (2005),[9] who also provide guidelines for designing appropriate incentives to mitigate such risks.

Potential risks in outsourcing can be further limited through judicious choices in product design. A modular architecture that enables plug and play capability also provides significant safeguards against outsourcing risks. In a fully decomposable product, individual components can be designed, maintained, and upgraded in isolation. Within this context, outsourced manufacturing of individual components presents limited risk. This, however, cannot be said for products with an integral architecture. Key trade-offs in organizational dependency and product decomposability are summarized in Table 3.4.[10] In the light of these trade-offs, a portfolio of buyer-supplier relationships should be developed.

Table 3.4 The matrix of organizational dependency and product modularity

Product Architecture	Dependent for Knowledge and Capacity	Dependent for Capacity Only
Item is Modular (Decomposable)	*A Potential Outsourcing Trap* Your partners could supplant you. They have as much or more knowledge and can obtain the same elements you can.	*Best Outsourcing Opportunity* You understand it, you can plug it into your process or product, and it probably can be obtained from several sources. It probably does not represent competitive advantage in and of itself. Buying it means you save attention to put into areas where you have competitive advantage.
Item is Integral (Not Decomposable)	*Worst Outsourcing Situation* You do not understand what you are buying or how to integrate it. The result could be failure since you will spend so much time on rework and rethinking.	*Can Live with Outsourcing* You know how to integrate the item so you may retain competitive advantage even if others have access to the same item.

3. Avoiding Surprises

3D-CE encourages the simultaneous consideration of these interfaces. Such concurrent engineering is, in turn, enabled by the architecture of the products, processes, and supply chains. Products can be
integral, embodying multiple functionalities (e.g., an aircraft wing),
or modular (decomposable), enabling independent design, maintenance, diagnostics, and upgrading (e.g., a PC). Processes can be dedicated (e.g., catalytic crackers) or flexible (e.g., a job shop). Supply
chains can be integral with tightly coupled processes (e.g., *Proton City*
in Malaysia, where all automotive suppliers are under the same roof
in a 5 million square meter facility with the final assembly line) or
modular with highly standardized interfaces (e.g., PC manufacturing
with global sourcing and channel assembly). In the long run, these
choices may support or hinder the dynamic evolution of supply
chain designs, as one faces new competition, new technologies, or
new legislation.

While one cannot fully anticipate the path of evolution in an
industry or the emergence of disruptive technologies, explicitly moni-
toring industry trends may provide valuable leading indicators. To
this end, a three-dimensional (3-D) supply chain mapping provides a
coherent framework to monitor organizational dependencies. In this
analysis, three maps of a business's value chain are constructed as
follows:[11]

1. *Organizational Supply Chain:* Taking either a product or a process
   view of your organization, enumerate first-tier suppliers who
   provide components or raw materials that your company uses to
   provide its products and services. Next, trace any connections
   that these suppliers may have with each other. Continue with
   the subsequent tiers.
2. *Technology Supply Chain:* This map is aimed at tracing the lines of
   dependency from your organization upstream and downstream to
   the suppliers and customers who provide and use the technologies
   that lie out of your immediate site. Drawing a map of key technologies deployed in the company's value chain helps you not
   only to visualize the connections between the technologies and
   your company's capabilities, but also to plan for alternatives if
   technologies fail or become unavailable.

3. *Business Capability Chain:* Identify and map key business process capabilities along the chain. This is the most conceptually challenging map.

Figure 3.8 shows a high-level mapping for the PC industry. *Hewlett-Packard (HP)*, which designs and sells PCs and servers as part of its complete IT solution offerings, purchases the microprocessors from *Intel*. In turn, *Intel* procures the photolithography equipment from *ASML*. At the heart of these wafer steppers are high-precision lenses produced by *Carl Zeiss*. Hence, these four organizations are not only members in an organizational supply chain, but they also participate in a technology and capability ecosystem. These ecosystems are complicated further by two-way dependencies. For example, *ASML* is not only a key supplier to *Intel*, but it also relies on *Intel* chips for the computer control of the equipment they design and build.

Using these three maps, the following questions for each element of the chain would provide valuable insights:

1. What is the clockspeed of this chain element and the industry in which it is embedded?
2. What factors (e.g., competition, technological innovation, regulations, etc.) are driving the clockspeed of this element?

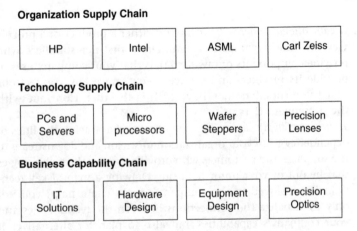

Figure 3.8 Mapping for organizational, technology, and capability chains.

3. What are the prospects for a change in clockspeed in this chain element as a result of expected changes in competitive intensity or in rates of innovation?
4. Where is the industry located on the double helix?
5. What are the current power dynamics for this element in the chain?

Referring back to the mapping in Figure 3.8, one can obtain further insights on this ecosystem by considering the varying clockspeeds across this chain. For instance, *HP* introduces a new PC every six months and a new server every nine months. Moore's Law, which asserts that the density (hence, the processing power) of a chip would double every 18 months, is pushing the physical limits of materials science, signaling a slow down in the introduction of ever more powerful microprocessors. A new process technology in chip making might totally change the configuration of this industry. Further upstream, the rate at which *ASML* introduces more advanced equipment that can produce chips with finer line width, which is largely driven by the availability of higher precision lenses, is definitely measured in years. On the other hand, the availability of a handful of photolithography equipment manufacturers and lens crafters should be a source of worry for all downstream consumers of these products.

An interesting complementary perspective on technology and business capability chains has recently been offered by Adner[12] within the context of innovation in ecosystems. In addition to the familiar 'initiative risk,' which reflects the likelihood of failing to reach the performance targets in internal projects undertaken by a company, Adner highlights two other complications in the supply chain: *interdependence risks*, the uncertainties of coordinating with complementary innovators; and *integration risks*, the uncertainties presented by the adoption process across the value chain. Suppose that, in Figure 3.8, *HP* wishes to develop a new server based on a newly designed *Intel* microprocessor. To be able to manufacture the processor, *Intel* would, in turn, depend on a new generation of photolithography equipment, developed by *ASML*, which would necessitate a sharper lens from *Zeiss*. Imagine that, based on the significant market potential, all four companies allocate significant resources to their individual projects, putting the likelihood of success for each stage at 90%. The likelihood that the new server would be successfully developed, however, is only 66% (0.90 * 0.90 * 0.90 * 0.90 = 0.66). In addition, if at any one stage, further complications arise and reduce the chance of successful development of that stage, the likelihood that the overall system succeeds becomes drastically lower. For example, if *ASML* encounters complications decreasing the likelihood of its success to 20%, the chances of success in developing the server sink to 15%. As Adner emphasizes, rather than judging whether or not this is too low of a number, one must focus on recognizing the interdependence risk and setting the correct expectations.

While the interdependence risk is multiplicative, the integration risk is additive. If *Zeiss* takes two years to develop the sharper lens, while *ASML*, *Intel*, and *HP* have five, four, and three years of design cycles, respectively, it would then take, at least, 2 + 5 + 4 + 3 = 14 years to get the new server to the market. One should not forget that adoption is viable at each stage only if the total cost of integrating the innovative components is smaller than the potential benefits at every stage. Yoffie and Kwak,[13] as well as Adner, suggest risk-mitigating strategies.

4. Summary

Just like products and processes, supply chain solutions have limited shelf life, where the life cycle is determined by an industry's clockspeed, the rate with which the industry's structure evolves. An industry's clockspeed may be measured based on the rate at which new products are introduced, based on the rate at which new processes are developed, or based on the rate new organizational relationships emerge. To avoid any unpleasant surprises, supply chain design should be viewed as a dynamic process, as "the capability to design and assemble assets, organizations, skill sets, and competencies for a *series* of competitive advantages, rather than a set of activities held together by low transaction costs." A 3-D supply chain mapping would prove valuable in signaling potential threats as well as new opportunities.

4
Value Creation:
Assessing the Cost-Service Trade-off

1. Motivation

In the previous chapter, we have emphasized the importance of product, process, and supply chain design in a dynamic environment where industry structures evolve continuously. While we have advocated a concurrent design approach along these three dimensions, one must resolve key cost-service trade-offs in each of those dimensions. In other words, one must assess whether investing in a product, process or supply chain redesign initiative is a value-creating or value-destroying proposition. For instance, if the increase in the customer's WTP due to the new product design is not sufficiently high to justify an investment of four man-months of additional research and development (R&D), this is a value-destroying proposal. To assess these trade-offs in an objective fashion, supply chain professionals need a simple but rich modelling tool. In this chapter, we formalize the cost-service trade-off, which affects supply chains, through a materials management framework. Such an inventory policy will not only allow us to quantify the cost-service trade-off, but will also identify (and cost out) principal levers one can deploy for mitigating such a trade-off.

1.1 Example: *FNAC*

FNAC is a leading French retailer of cultural products such as books, CDs, and DVDs as well as electronics such as PCs, MP3 players, and plasma TVs. On the one hand, *FNAC*'s marketing strategy is strongly anchored on the wide portfolio of cultural products it offers to its customers. On the other hand, *FNAC* operates stores in urban locations where real estate is extremely expensive, necessitating the efficient use of every square meter. This, in turn, puts a tight constraint on the amount of inventory each retail outlet can hold. In guiding its decisions on store assortment, the retailer must therefore carefully assess the consequences of satisfying the following four business criteria:

1. Criticality of product availability:
   a. Product contribution
   b. Product appeal
2. Ease of demand forecasting:
   a. Average demand rate
   b. Demand volatility
3. Supplier capability:
   a. Operational flexibility
   b. Logistical flexibility
4. Risk in stocking the product:
   a. Obsolescence
   b. Physical characteristics

FNAC takes pride in offering a wide variety of books, CDs, DVDs, and electronics. It would be unthinkable for the retailer not to have a great French classic novel, a current best seller, or a popular video game on its shelves. This is the first dimension of the criticality of product availability. The second dimension is about margins; hardbound books, video games, and latest electronic gadgets certainly have attractive margins compared to paperbacks. The second criterion is focused on assessing sales volumes and sales volatility. It is relatively easier to forecast sales of Victor Hugo's classic books; however, sales of a new book might flare up after the announcement of a literary prize and die down as rapidly within days. The third criterion focuses on the ease of replenishment. An out-of-stock book in French can be replenished within 24 hours if the publisher has the book in inventory (high logistical flexibility); however, if the publisher is out-of-stock, then long replenishment lead times are to be expected as the publisher may not immediately print another batch of the popular book (low operational flexibility). On the other hand, if the out-of-stock product is a video game, it would be a matter of minutes to burn new CDs (high operational flexibility). However, if the supplier is in Japan, this would necessitate a shipping delay of six weeks (low logistical flexibility). The last criterion is about the "cube" that occupies expensive shelf space.

A cell phone, which may become obsolete in a few weeks, has a relatively small footprint. A plasma television set, on the other hand, not only becomes obsolete in a few months, but also takes up a lot of expensive real estate. *FNAC* must therefore design and deploy affordable supply chain solutions to support the above four business criteria. As a prerequisite, *FNAC* must be able to assess the associated cost-service trade-off.

2. A base stock policy

To formally define an inventory policy, consider the scenario depicted in Figure 4.1, where on-hand inventory is used to meet customer demand that occurs in a random fashion. Inventory is replenished by placing orders at the supplier, who produces and delivers the requested quantity after a given lead time. Note that we distinguish *on-hand inventory* from *inventory position*. The latter is the sum of on-hand inventory and the *pipeline inventory*, material ordered but not yet delivered, less any *outstanding backorders*. In this scenario, we need to answer three questions:

- How frequently do we review the inventory levels?
- How frequently do we place a replenishment order?
- What is the replenishment quantity?

The answer to these three questions constitutes an inventory policy. In the absence of any fixed ordering (transaction) costs, a base stock (or order-up-to-S, where S is the base stock level) policy has been shown to be optimal. Base stock policies are easy to define and implement: for every p periods, an order for a sufficient number of units is

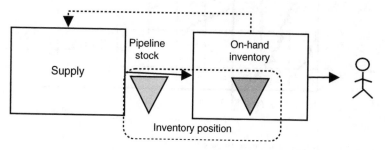

Figure 4.1   A simple supply chain.

placed so as to bring the inventory position up to S. In this setting, the frequency with which we review the on-hand inventory and the frequency with which we place orders are fixed. This assumption may represent a situation whereby the supplier's own planning cycle is imposing a constraint on the frequency of replenishment orders that can be placed by the customer. There is, however, flexibility in the order quantity, which reflects the intensity of the demand during the replenishment cycle.

Assume that the demand distribution, along with its mean and variance, is known. The replenishment leadtime, say l, is a known constant. As shown in Figure 4.2, for every p periods, we will review the inventory level and place an order for a quantity that would restore the inventory position up to the base stock level, S. What is then the optimal base stock level?

Note that if there was no variability in the demand, one would place an order for the quantity that would satisfy the total demand during the replenishment lead time, namely for $\mu(p+l)$ quantity (where μ is the daily demand for the product, p is the time period of the inventory level, and l is the replenishment lead time). In other words, if we reviewed our inventory level every week with a replenishment lead time of two days and a daily demand of 10 units, we would need $10*(7+2) = 90$ units to fully satisfy the (deterministic)

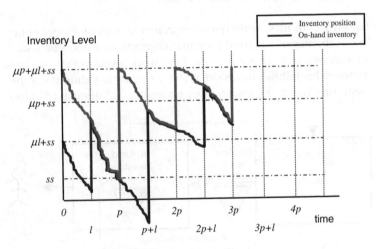

Figure 4.2   A base stock inventory system.

demand during the replenishment cycle. Hence, we would set our order-up-to level to 90. When demand is random, our short-term solution is to place some safety stock to absorb such fluctuations; i.e., buffer or suffer (from fluctuations). For example, in the first replenishment cycle in Figure 4.2, the observed demand exceeded the expected demand; there was, however, a sufficient amount of safety stock to satisfy this additional demand. In the second cycle, the observed demand was so high that we not only used up all the safety stock, but also ended up losing sales. In the third cycle, on the other hand, the observed demand way below our expectations. In such a scenario, where we have to accommodate demand fluctuations, we set the order-up-to level to S, where

$$S = \text{expected demand during replenishment lead time} \\ + \text{safety stock}$$

that is

$$S = \mu(p+l) + \text{safety stock}.$$

We then need to determine the right level of safety stock. Before we develop an adequate expression, let us determine the drivers of safety stock. There are four key drivers:

- The volatility of demand, σ
- The replenishment lead time, l
- The length of the review period, p
- The desired customer service level, z

Putting these drivers together, the order-up-to level is given by:

$$S = \mu(p+l) + z\sigma\sqrt{p+l},$$

where the first part of the equation represents the expected demand during the replenishment lead time, whereas the second part is the safety stock kept to accommodate demand fluctuations.

In the expression for base stock S, the average demand as well as its volatility can be estimated from historical data. Similarly, the length of the review period and replenishment lead time is typically dictated by the production and distribution constraints. It therefore remains to determine the multiplier, z, that reflects the desired customer service level. Here, we have two possibilities. One can invoke the newsvendor scenario,[1] if a good estimate of the overage and underage costs (c_o and c_u, respectively) exists. In that case, the ratio of the overage cost to the total cost of demand supply mismatch yields the critical fractile, and z is determined by inverting the demand distribution $F(x) \equiv Prob\{D \leqslant x\}$:

$$z = F^{-1}\left(\frac{c_u}{c_u + c_o}\right).$$

If we are willing to assume that demand is distributed according to a Normal distribution with mean μ and standard deviation σ, we can use the table in Appendix A to obtain the corresponding z value. Alternatively, the Excel function NORMSINV provides the necessary multiplier:

$$z = \text{NORMSINV}(c_o / c_u + c_o).$$

The newsvendor scenario will be formally introduced in the next chapter. In this scenario, the cost of overage is typically easy to estimate reflecting the cost of holding excess stock, the opportunity cost of money tied up to excess stock or the risk of obsolescence. The cost of underage, on the other hand, is harder to obtain as it reflects not only the foregone margin at present, but also the loss of customer goodwill in the long run. In such cases, we need an alternative approach to determine the multiplier, z. One alternative is to start with a targeted customer service level, measured by, say, fill rates, f, and then determine the multiplier that would achieve the desired service level. To this end, the supply chain specialist would benchmark competing firms with respect to the service levels they offer or would consult with their marketing colleagues regarding the service levels expected by their customers. For example, *HP* requires relatively high fill rates for its laser printers, as the installed product base is the primary driver of high-margin consumables such as replacement cartridges, paper, and service contracts. Similarly, *Coloplast*, a Danish wound-care products manufacturer, requires that fill rates for hospitals be nearly 100%, as they discovered that a patient who leaves the hospital with a *Coloplast* product is highly likely to remain loyal by continuing to purchase the same brand throughout his treatment.

How do we then translate the desired service level, expressed in terms of the fill rate f, into the multiplier z? Technically, we choose z such that

$$f = 1 - \frac{L(z)\sigma\sqrt{p+l}}{\mu p},$$

where, the quantity $L(z)$ is called the *standard loss function*. The standard loss function is also provided in the Appendix. In technical terms, this is a *conditional* expectation: the average demand during the replenishment lead time *given* that the demand exceeds the safety stock. This quantity therefore represents the average lost sales during the replenishment lead time. The denominator, on the other hand, reflects the average demand during a review period. The ratio then yields the proportion of lost sales during this cycle; one minus that ratio is therefore equal to the fill rate.

Rearranging the terms, we obtain

$$L(z) = (1-f)\frac{\mu p}{\sigma\sqrt{p+l}}.$$

If we further assume that the demand follows a Normal distribution, we can use the table in the Appendix to determine the corresponding z value, enabling us to compute the order-up-to level through

$$S = \mu(p+l) + z\sigma\sqrt{p+l}.$$

2.1 Example continued: FNAC

Before we run some numbers, let us revisit the *FNAC* example and see how the retailer's customer service criteria can be mapped onto the base stock model to assess the associated cost-service trade-off. The first criterion, criticality of product availability, is directly related to the fill rate, f, that must be set in accordance with the marketing goals. The second criterion, ease of demand forecasting, is reflected by μ and σ in the model. The third criterion, supplier capability, is illustrated by p, which, as the review frequency, reflects its operational flexibility, and by l, which, as the replenishment lead time, reflects its logistical flexibility. Finally, the risk of obsolescence and the stockability of the "cube" can be reflected through the selected fill rate, *f*. FNAC can then assess the cost-service trade-off inherent in various possible supply chain solutions (e.g., centralizing the inventory of a certain product family at a distribution center versus pushing the product to the shelves of a retail outlet).

2.2 Running the numbers

Consider the following scenario. Suppose that you are selling a product whose forecast calls for an average demand level of 150 units per week with a standard deviation of 50 units per week, representing the volatility of demand. As an internal policy, inventory is reviewed every other week (p = 2 weeks). The supplier quotes a production and delivery lead time of 1 week (l = 1 week). The marketing strategy calls for a high level of customer service, expressed in terms of the desired fill rate: f = 0.99. The base stock level that achieves the desired service kevel can be calculated as follows:

$$\text{Cycle stock} = \mu p/2 = 150 \cdot 2/2 = 150 \text{ units}$$

$$\text{Pipeline stock} = \mu l = 150 \cdot 1 = 150 \text{ units}$$

We can then calculate the base stock level through:

$$L(z) = (1-f)\frac{\mu p}{\sigma\sqrt{p+l}} = (.01)\frac{150 \cdot 2}{10\sqrt{2}+1} = 0.173,$$

so from the appendix, z = 0.58

$$S = \mu p + \mu l + z\sigma\sqrt{p+l} = 150 \cdot 2 + 150 \cdot 1 + .58 \cdot 10\sqrt{3} = 460.$$

This simple framework provides an objective platform to quantify the cost-service trade-off. Note that, in this expression, the key drivers of inventory are the following:

- the review frequency, p
- the production and distribution lead time, l
- the expected demand rate, μ
- the volatility of the demand, σ
- the service requirements expressed through the multiplier, z

In a given supply chain, each of these drivers can be the subject of negotiations among the involved stakeholders. For example, a manufacturer might ask its supplier to modify the frequency with which he can place replenishment orders, i.e., *p*. As such, added flexibility will decrease the required inventory investment (hence, the WCR) by the manufacturer in a quantifiable fashion, some of those savings can be passed along to the supplier as an incentive to provide such flexibility. In a similar fashion, the value of reducing the lead times, *l*, can be assessed. For example, such a calculation would help us to assess whether shipping by airfreight overnight makes sense compared to shipping by sea over six weeks. Or, if the firm is considering alternative investments to reduce demand volatility, this expression enables a quick cost-benefit analysis between the investments required to reduce volatility and the reduced reliance on safety stocks due to lower volatility. Finally, if the marketing department insists on a certain service level, this expression provides the cost of providing the desired service.

In fact, by considering different service levels, one can generate a cost-service trade-off curve, as illustrated in Figure 4.3. Such a curve would provide further help in segmenting the target market by offering premium (and more costly) service to top customers.

Supply chain professionals can make a sustainable difference, however, by designing products, processes, and supply chains that would shift the trade-off curve, hence mitigating the cost-service trade-off. Postponement strategies represent one such instrument that would mitigate the cost-service trade-off. In fact, Figure 4.3 is based on the *HP* Deskjet printer's supply chain case study.[2] The case illustrates an

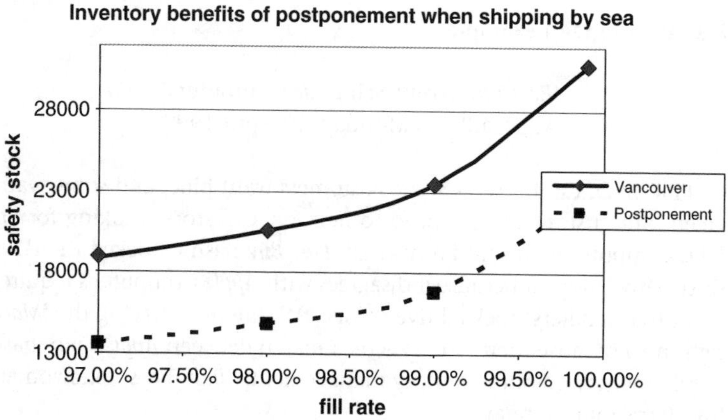

Figure 4.3 The cost-service trade-off curve for *HP* Deskjet printers.

inventory-service crisis, where product variety driven by localization requirements (e.g., power supply, software and manuals in the appropriate language) overwhelms the capabilities of the *HP* Deskjet printer's supply chain. Despite a state-of-the-art JIT factory in Vancouver, Washington, *HP* was not able to forecast the product demand accurately, resulting in severe stock-outs in some markets, while inventory built up in others. Within the base stock framework, supply chain experts at *HP* were able to assess the cost-service trade-off among various supply chain solutions such as shipping products through air freight (reducing *l* but drastically increasing transportation costs), building another factory in Europe (reducing both *p* and *l* but necessitating a major capital investment) or boosting safety stock levels (increasing WCR while hoping to achieve higher fill rates).

The solution that was ultimately adopted (and became a benchmark in many other industries) is *delayed customization* or *postponement*, whereby the Vancouver plant would produce the hardware based on forecasts, which would ultimately be customized in a distribution center close to the customer (preferably after a firm customer order has been received). The cost-service trade-off curve under the postponement strategy is also reflected in Figure 4.3 with the broken line. *HP* managers were then able to quantify the savings due to postponement and assess whether the investment in product and supply chain redesign to enable delayed customization capability was indeed a value-creating proposal. Today, postponement is done through a third-party logistics service provider for *HP* in Europe.

2.3 An extended example

"Best Buy Won't Sell *iMac* Computers"
AP Headlines Monday, 19 April 1999

CUPERTINO, Calif. (AP) – Some customers want blue, and some want green. But customers who head to *Best Buy* Co. stores looking for an *iMac* computer won't find any at all. *Best Buy* hasn't stocked the *iMac* since early this year because it disagrees with *Apple* Computer's requirement that retailers stock all five colors. "We are not carrying the *iMacs* right now because there isn't exactly a match between *Apple*'s purchase requirements and our inventory management," *Best Buy* spokeswoman Joy Harris said Monday.

The $1,199 computers, on store shelves in five colors since January, have been most popular in blueberry and grape. The lime, tangerine and strawberry models have been less popular. *Apple* recently shifted its policy, shipping four blues with one of each of the other colors. "We're definitely trying to work this out," said *Apple* spokeswoman Rhona Hamilton. So far, the adjustments aren't working for *Best Buy*. The company did not specify which colors it does not want to stock.

Other computer stores said Monday they do not have a problem with *Apple*'s policy. Suzanne Shelton at Dallas-based CompUSA, said the purple models, dubbed "grape," have been very popular. But she said that when those run out on store shelves, customers are content to buy whatever is in stock. "Some of them are faster sellers than others," she said, "but so far that hasn't proven to be a real problem for us." A clerk at one California Fry's Electronics chain, where the shelves held plenty of blueberries and no tangerine, strawberry, lime or grape models, said customers will take what they can get.

Best Buy, which has 300 stores in 36 states, may eventually stock the *iMacs*, Harris said. "It's just taking a lot of negotiation," she said.

Assume the following, if *Best Buy* were to purchase the *iMac* from *Apple* Computer:

- Average demand for a Blueberry (Blue) *iMac* at a typical *Best Buy* store would be 40 units per week with a standard deviation of demand of 10 units per week.
- Average demand for a Tangerine (Orange) *iMac* at a typical *Best Buy* store would be 10 units per week with a standard deviation of demand of 5 units per week.
- *Best Buy* would place weekly orders for *iMacs* to *Apple*.
- Shipments would arrive from *Apple* two weeks after the orders were placed by *Best Buy*.
- *Best Buy* has a target line item fill rate of 99%.
- *Best Buy* would purchase *iMacs* (all colors) from *Apple* for $1,100 per unit.
- *Best Buy*'s inventory carrying cost for computers is 50% of product cost per year.

Consider the inventory levels for Blueberry *iMacs* at the typical store if *Best Buy* uses the periodic review, order-up-to policy.

Inventory levels for *Blueberry iMACs* can be calculated as follows:

- Cycle stock = $\mu p/2 = 40 \times 1/2 = 20$
- Pipeline stock = $\mu l = 40 \times 2 = 80$
- Safety stock = $z\sigma\sqrt{p+l}$ in which z is determined by using the Standard Loss Function/Standard Normal Table using formula: $L(z) = (1-f) * (\mu p / \sigma\sqrt{p+l})$.

$$L(z) = (1-0.99) * (40 * 1/10\sqrt{2+1}) = 0.01 * (40/10\sqrt{3}) = 0.02309.$$

From the appendix, the z value is 1.6. Hence, the safety stock level is given by:

$$SS = z\sigma\sqrt{p+l} = 1.6 * 10\sqrt{2+1} = 27.7 \approx 28.$$

The base stock level is then given by:

$$S = \mu(p+l) + z\sigma\sqrt{p+l} = 40 + 80 + 28 = 148 \text{ units.}$$

Consider the inventory levels for Tangerine *iMacs* at the typical store if Best Buy uses the periodic review, order-up-to policy.

Inventory levels for Tangerine *iMACs* can be calculated as follows:

- Cycle stock = $\mu p/2 = 10 * 1/2 = 5$
- Pipeline stock = $\mu l = 10 * 2 = 20$
- Safety stock = $z\sigma\sqrt{p+l}$ in which z is determined by using the Standard Loss Function/Standard Normal Table using formula: $L(z) = (1-f) * (\mu p / \sigma\sqrt{p+l})$.

Thus,

$$L(z) = (1-0.99) * (10 * 1/5\sqrt{2+1}) = 0.01 * (10/5\sqrt{3}) = 0.01155.$$

From the appendix the z value is 1.9. Hence, the safety stock level is given by:

$$SS = z\sigma\sqrt{p+l} = 1.9 * 5\sqrt{2+1} = 16.45 \approx 17.$$

The base stock level is then given by:

$$S = \mu(p+l) + z\sigma\sqrt{p+l} = 10 + 20 + 17 = 47 \text{ units.}$$

A marketing executive suggests that *Best Buy* might carry the *iMac* in all colors if *Apple* would offer a per-unit discount on less popular colors to offset the higher effective inventory-carrying cost per unit sold for less popular colors. Based on the above calculations, what per-unit discount should *Apple* offer to *Best Buy* for Tangerine computers in order to make them indifferent between selling computers in Tangerine and Blueberry? (Assume that Blueberry computers will be sold to *Best Buy* at $1,100/unit. *You may also assume that Best Buy does not take ownership of computers until they arrive at the retail stores.*)

To calculate the appropriate level of compensation, we need to first determine the inventory carrying costs for the two computers. For the Blueberry, the average annual inventory carrying cost is given by

$$(20 + 28 \text{ units}) * (\$1100/\text{unit}) * 0.50 = \$24,600 \text{ per annum.}$$

For Tangerine, the average annual inventory carrying cost is given by

$$(5 + 17) * (\$1100/\text{unit}) * 0.50 = \$12,100 \text{ per annum.}$$

These numbers, however, are not directly comparable, because the two computers have different annual sales volumes. We could use the annual sales volume to normalize the numbers and make them directly comparable. Assuming a 50-week year, the sales volume for Blueberry is $40 * 50 = 2000$ units/year whereas the sales volume for Tangerine is $10 * 50 = 500$ units/year.

The inventory carrying charge per unit sold is then given by:

$$\text{Blueberry: } \$24,600/2000 = \$13.20$$

$$\text{Tangerine: } \$12,100/500 = \$24.20$$

The compensation should then be based on the extra cost of carrying Tangerines in inventory, $\Delta = \$24.20 - \$13.20 = \$11$.

3. Long-term solutions

The base stock model that was introduced to quantify the cost-service trade-off can also be viewed as one short-term solution to inventory management challenges. From this materials management perspective, it is worthwhile to open a parenthesis here to seek longer term solutions. A long-term orientation, in return, requires the identification of inventory drivers, business conditions, and constraints that necessitate inventory holding. Unless these drivers are eliminated through better product, process, or supply chain design, stockless production and distribution is not possible. To this end, there are several ways of classifying inventories. Frustrated supply chain professionals may classify them as SLOBS (slow moving or obsolete stocks) or as FISH (first in still here). Accountants classify inventories as raw materials, work-in-process or finished goods for reporting purposes. However, instead of using any of the above classifications, we will introduce a *dynamic classification scheme* that highlights the underlying drivers. One should note that the purpose is not to walk through a manufacturing facility or a warehouse and label various kinds of stocks encountered along the way. The idea is to simply highlight the principal operating condition that necessitates inventory holding. One should also note that while we will describe the key drivers individually, they typically occur simultaneously with a compounding effect on the business. Our purpose in introducing them individually, however, is to emphasize the trade-offs they each induce on the operations of a supply chain.

The most obvious reason why inventories cannot be avoided is that production and distribution are not instantaneous (pipeline stocks). Seasonal inventories are built to absorb variations in supply and/or demand. Due to transaction costs, it is more economical to order or produce more than one unit of any particular item at a time (cycle stocks). Safety stocks are built as a hedge against uncertainty in demand or supply. Decoupling stocks are held between two stages of production in order to absorb variations in the production rates of the two stages. We will therefore classify inventories into the following categories:

- Pipeline stocks
- Seasonal stocks
- Cycle stocks
- Safety stocks
- Decoupling stocks

For a more detailed discussion, consider the following scenarios.

Pipeline stocks:

A wine grower sells on average 1000 bottles of wine per year. The grower, however, will not sell the wine until it is aged for four years. To sustain his sales volume of 1000 bottles per year, how much of a pipeline inventory must the grower maintain?

This scenario is best described by one of the key models in Operations Management: *Little's Law*,[3] which states:

System Stock (L) = System Throughput (λ) × System Lead Time (W)

In our case, since the desired throughput is sales of 1000 bottles per year and because the grower insists on four years of aging, he must then carry, at any given point in time, a pipeline stock of 4000 bottles (=1000 bottles per year × 4 years).

Disciples of the JIT movement would readily recognize Little's Law as the keystone of kanban control. In kanban-controlled pull systems, to achieve a predictable production lead time, manufacturing engineers design a production process with a certain throughput rate and then limit system stock by controlling the number of kanban cards in circulation. In other words, by fixing L and λ, they determine the lead time, W, as $W = L/\lambda$.

Seasonal stocks:

Consider a toy manufacturer who sells 12,000 toy trucks a year. The manufacturer has a plant with a capacity of 1000 trucks per month. Unfortunately, sales are slow during the year and peaks during the Christmas season. More specifically, the manufacturer sells 100 trucks/month in January through November, while the sales reach 10,900 trucks in December. There are two basic possibilities to match demand and supply. The first one requires a highly flexible manufacturing process that can produce 100 trucks per month for 11 months out of the year and then increase the production rate to 10,900 trucks/month for one month. Not many production processes offer such levels of flexibility. The remaining possibility is therefore to build ahead and accumulate stock ahead of the sales season by steadily producing at capacity. This is depicted in Figure 4.4 for the production capacity of 1000 trucks per month. At any given point in time, the vertical difference between cumulative production and cumulative sales corresponds to seasonal stock.

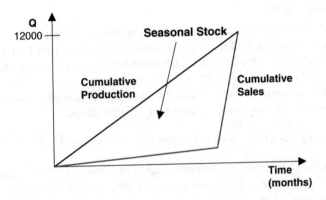

Figure 4.4   The impact of seasonal demand for toys: seasonal stocks.

This phenomenon is quite common in services as well. A hotel with 500 rooms may experience an occupancy rate of 100% during the summer months (high season), but may only be 40% full during the winter months. The difference between the maximum capacity and the occupancy rate may then be viewed as seasonal stock (of guest rooms).

Perhaps the most appropriate use of this label is in agriculture. For example, in the northern hemisphere, apples are harvested in August and September, placed in climate-controlled sealed rooms, and sold throughout the year. The content of the sealed rooms at any point during the year represents seasonal stocks.

Cycle stocks:

A chocolate junkie devours one chocolate bar a day. She has the following choices: she can go to the grocery store every morning and purchase a bar of chocolate to eat that afternoon or she can visit the grocery store on Monday morning and get seven bars of chocolate to last her the entire week. What is her optimal policy?

Our chocolate lover faces a basic trade-off between the cost of visiting the grocery store (gasoline consumption and the wear and tear on the car due to driving, the opportunity cost of her time, etc.) and the cost of holding seven chocolate bars in inventory. As illustrated in Figure 4.5, if she stops by the grocery store every day and purchases just one bar for immediate consumption, she will incur this 'set up cost' every day while holding no inventory. On the other hand, if she

Figure 4.5 Cycle stocks and the EOQ.

only goes shopping once and purchases all seven chocolate bars, she will end up incurring the set-up cost once, but will have to hold inventory throughout the week. This trade-off is addressed by one of the classical models in Operations Management, *Wilson's square root formula*[4] (also known as the *Economic Order Quantity* [EOQ]). EOQ yields the optimal order quantity in the presence of a fixed set-up and a linear holding cost as follows:

$$Q^* = \sqrt{\frac{2DS}{h}},$$

where D is the demand rate (7 bars per week), S is the set-up cost, and h is the holding cost.

The EOQ reflects the optimal purchase (or production) quantity when faced with a trade-off between set-up cost and inventory holding cost. Q^* is the quantity that minimizes the sum of these two conflicting cost drivers. While myopic, EOQ has several desirable characteristics that make it a widely used inventory model in practice. First, it is a very robust model: for example, if one commits a 100% error in forecasting the demand, the resulting error in the purchase quantity is only 40% due to the square root. Second, it clearly depicts intuitive economic relationships. For instance, if machine set ups are long, creating a lot of costly down time in a manufacturing facility, EOQ advocates large production batch sizes. (It is therefore not surprising that a key pillar of the JIT philosophy is on reducing set-up times, making it economically feasible to produce in small quantities and to switch frequently among different product families.) On the other hand, if holding cost is very large (say, due to high obsolescence risk), EOQ advocates production or procurement in small quantities.

Safety stocks:

You are planning a birthday party for your seven-year old. The key question is how big of a birthday cake to make. In the past, ten school friends showed up, on average, for the festivities. Last year, however, 15 kids were at the party. If you make a cake for 15 and only 10 kids show up, that would be a waste. If, on the other hand, you make a cake for 10 and all 15 kids show up, that would be an embarrassment. What should you do?

To be able to answer this question, one has to estimate the economic impact of the demand-supply mismatch. In case demand exceeds supply, we end up incurring an "underage" cost. In the reverse case, where supply exceeds demand, we have an "overage" cost. The former may include not only the foregone margin, but also some loss in customer goodwill. The latter may include the production or purchase cost as well as any cost associated with disposing of excess stock. The framework that determines a quantity, which maximized the expected profit in this uncertain environment, is the *newsvendor model*. This model is introduced in detail in the next chapter and deployed in the context of value capture.

Decoupling stocks:

In a factory producing washing machines, an automated manufacturing cell produces 8 shells per shift. Further downstream, these shells are assembled manually into washing machines at a rate of 12 machines per shift. Driven by technological constraints, production and assembly, therefore, require careful coordination. As illustrated in Figure 4.6, the output from the automated manufacturing cell overnight (during the graveyard shift) has to be stored in a buffer between production and manual assembly. In the absence of such

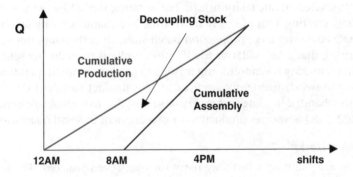

Figure 4.6 Coordinating production and assembly through decoupling stocks.

decoupling stock, either the automated manufacturing cell may be blocked or the manual assembly process may be starved, resulting in throughput loss for the overall production facility.

A fruit processing plant cleans and sorts freshly picked apples that farmers bring from their orchards. It is the plant's policy to start receiving the fruit at 7 a.m., but not to start the processing until 9 a.m. This policy attempts to decouple a very stable processing operation inside the plant from a highly volatile external arrival process through the accumulation of fresh fruit over a two-hour period. Such decoupling stocks play a crucial role in petrochemical complex where starving operations due to a disruption in feedstock has huge economic consequences due to high restart costs.

Just like a fever is a symptom of an underlying infection, inventories are symptoms of underlying operational constraints. For example, pipeline stocks are needed since there is a nonnegligible lead time for production and distribution. In our wine example, one way to cut pipeline stock is to age the wine for a shorter period of time. This is exactly what *Beaujolais Nouveau* does in France. With grapes that are harvested at the end of August, wine is bottled in October; the fresh wine is then sold on the third Thursday of November with a great marketing push. Similarly, seasonal stocks are needed, as capacity is too rigid to catch up with the demand. Demand management aimed at increasing the demand during the low season (e.g., preferential pricing) is a possible remedy. This topic is further discussed in Chapter 7, where service supply chains are analyzed.

Cycle stocks are carried, as set-up costs are nonnegligible. One of the key ingredients of the JIT movement was to reduce set-up times so that batch sizes (hence, cycle stocks) can be reduced. Safety stocks will be indispensable as long as uncertainty cannot be eliminated. In certain cases, it may be more economical to simply hold safety stocks than to try to eliminate all sources of uncertainty. Decoupling stocks are necessitated by variability and demand-supply imbalance. Synchronization through better process design is a long-term remedy.

The bottom line is that unless one is capable of addressing the drivers of inventory, zero inventories will be neither desirable nor achievable. Our dynamic classification of inventories along with the short-term trade-offs, underlying causes, and potential long-term remedies are summarized in Table 4.1.

Table 4.1   Drivers of inventory

Type of Stock	Short-Term Trade-offs	Underlying Causes	Suggested Remedies
Pipeline Stocks	None	Lead time	Relayout Colocation
Seasonal Stocks	Capacity utilization Lost sales	Seasonal demand Rigid capacity	Demand management Flexible capacity
Cycle Stocks	Set-up costs Fixed ordering costs	Lack of flexibility Product variety	Quick set ups Focused product lines
Safety Stocks	Backorders Lost sales	Uncertainty Lead time	POS data Express delivery
Decoupling Stocks	Capacity utilization Throughput	Variability Imbalance	Reliability Synchronization

4. Summary

- A base stock policy is not just an easy-to-define-and-implement materials management system, but also a transparent way of establishing the cost-service trade-off.
- The immediate use of the trade-off curve is in segmenting the target customer base with "A" customers receiving higher levels of service (measured in this case by the fill rate), naturally at a higher cost. For "B" customers, one can then reduce both the service levels and the corresponding cost to serve.
- The real value that supply chain professionals add, however, is in redesigning products, processes, and supply chain interfaces so that the trade-off curve shifts out to the left, representing a mitigation of the cost-service trade-off. The model is then useful in quantifying the resulting savings and assessing whether the investment necessary in generating this shift makes financial sense (i.e., has a positive NPV).

5
Value Capture: Aligning the Supply Chain Partners

1. Motivation

In the PC industry, it is customary to talk about the "smiley curve." The x-axis of the curve shows the various players in this supply chain, namely equipment makers, manufacturers of microprocessors and other components, PC assemblers, distributors, value-added resellers, and service providers. The y-axis reflects the margins made (i.e., the value captured) by each of these players. The "smiley curve" asserts that while both the upstream (e.g., equipment and micro-processor manufacturers) and downstream players (e.g., service providers) make healthy margins, PC assemblers' margins are relatively thin. A similar challenge is also present in service industries. Consider, for example, the airline industry. Over the past few years, while airlines have been struggling to avoid bankruptcy or trying to climb back out of it, aircraft manufacturers, aircraft leasing companies, reservation systems, and airport operators have achieved respectable financial results. Hence, the value captured by different players varies drastically along this supply chain as well. There are many other examples where the value created by the entire supply chain is captured in an uneven fashion by the different players in that ecosystem.

Value capture was less of a challenge when vertical integration was the dominant industry structure. As an extreme example, one can consider the *Ford Corporation* in the early 20th century, where *Ford* owned and operated every echelon of their supply chain from iron mines to car dealerships. In such a setting, a single "control tower" used to manage both value creation and value capture for the entire ecosystem. Current industry structure, however, is anything but vertically integrated. From cars to computers, airplanes to consumer goods, entertainment to electronics, every echelon of these supply chains are owned and operated by independent organizations. In other words, a single systemwide management structure with clear command and control responsibilities has been replaced by multiple rational economic agents with possibly divergent – even conflicting – interests and priorities. The challenge has therefore become the alignment and coordination of these independent agents.

We will address this challenge in this chapter. We will first introduce some working definitions. We will then discuss the consequences of misalignment. Both long-term and short-term initiatives to achieve coordination will be introduced; implementation challenges will be discussed.

2. Challenges in supply chain coordination

The key consequence of the lack of *supply chain coordination* is the *bullwhip phenomenon*. As depicted in Figure 5.1, this is the amplification of volatility along the network, that is, the increase in demand variability as one moves upstream farther and farther away from the market. The key drivers of the bullwhip phenomenon include the lack of information sharing, communication, and collaboration among the supply chain entities as well as physical delays in information and material flows. In other words, any change in the marketplace, when coupled with information distortions and information and physical

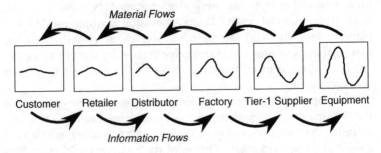

Figure 5.1   The bullwhip phenomenon.

delays, results in increasing levels of volatility as we travel upstream along the supply chain.

Rather than trying to boost forecast accuracy or reduce market volatility, any initiative that promotes higher supply chain transparency by eliminating information delays and distortions through information sharing and achieves enhanced agility by shortening physical delays would go a long way in mitigating the bullwhip. With the ubiquity of the Internet, information delays are easier to eliminate – provided that there is a willingness to share information. Physical delays, however, are more difficult to overcome, both in the manufacturing and service domains, as discussed within the context of pipeline inventories in the previous chapter.

Coordination is further hampered by structural constraints that favor local optimization.[1] Consider the practices of order batching, shortage gaming, forward buying, and demand forecast updating. Order batching distorts and delays information. For example, a retailer observing daily sales, typically places replenishment orders on a weekly or monthly basis. In this case, the orders that the supplier receives are both aggregated, hence, distorted, and delayed. However, there are some economic reasons for batching orders. First, it is costly to process orders. (Recall the discussion at the end of the previous chapter on the ordering or set-up costs within the context of the Wilson's square root formula.) An organization or information infrastructure must be maintained to receive and process the requirements. Second, there are economies of scale in transportation: a full truckload is cheaper than partial shipments. Hence, even if the retailer wishes to replenish what was sold on a given day, the supplier may not be willing to send a (partially loaded) truck to that outlet. Finally, there may be some sales incentives for purchasing in larger quantities. Given these (local) constraints, it may be more economical to simply batch orders.

Shortage gaming is another big driver of the bullwhip, plaguing particularly electronics and toy manufacturers. For example, toy retailers, who achieve the biggest proportion of their annual sales during the Christmas season, tend to overstate their forecasts to ensure sufficient inventory for this vital selling season. This, in turn, sends an exaggerated signal to manufacturers, who may choose to (erroneously) increase production thinking that there is great market demand for their products.

Forward buying is a prevalent practice in the grocery industry, where margins are razor thin. Some studies point out that 80% of the transactions between manufacturers and distributors are done on a forward buying basis, where items are bought in advance of actual requirements to take advantage of reduced purchase prices. Since this inventory is pushed on to the channel ahead of the actual demand realization, the market picture is further distorted.

Demand forecast updating is also commonplace: the manufacturing department receives a demand forecast from the sales department. Just to be on the safe side, they inflate the forecast by 10% before sending it to their suppliers. To be further on the safe side, the supplier revises the forecast upward by another 10%, etc. As the updated forecast travels upstream along the supply chain, the figures that the last supplier sees are totally detached from the market realities that the sales department tried to capture in its original forecast.

In each of these cases, the decision maker has acted in an economically rational fashion, managing his/her own risk, ultimately making a locally optimal decision. In the absence of a clear command and control structure, however, simply collating these locally optimal decisions together along the supply chain does not yield a globally optimal solution for the entire chain. Instead it leads to chaos, which is labelled as 'the bullwhip phenomenon' in a politically correct fashion. The key challenge is, therefore, to promote such collaborative practices that would minimize supply chain disruptions and maximize supply chain profits.

3. Achieving supply chain collaboration

As discussed in the previous chapter, *HP* introduced the Deskjet printer two decades ago. Combining the quality of laser printers with the affordability of dot matrix printers, the product was a stellar success with sales volumes exceeding even the most optimistic forecasts around the world. There was, however, a simple problem. Based on the initial assessments of the market potential, *HP* had decided to dedicate a single production facility for manufacturing Deskjet printers. *HP* sales organizations around the world would send their forecasts to the single factory at Vancouver and the factory would produce the printers JIT based on these forecasts. But the forecasts were never accurate, leading into an inventory-service crisis. While one country was overflowing with inventory, another one was experiencing severe shortages. A task force that was put together to defuse the crisis considered several options, including shipments through airfreight, a second factory, and higher levels of channel inventory. Ultimately, the postponement idea was adopted based on the calculations illustrated in the previous chapter. Under postponement, the factory would produce and ship the hardware based on forecasts. The hardware would then be customized upon the receipt of a customer order. To enable this postponement strategy, several modifications had to be made to the product and to the supply chain. The product design had to be modified so that the power unit could be taken out of the printer so as to enable plug and play. As for the supply chain, the loading of the software in the correct language as well as the final testing would be done in a field warehouse instead of the manufacturing site. While the cost-service trade-off associated with postponement was clearly quantified, the roll out of the idea that necessitated the buy-in from all the stakeholders turned out to be a completely different challenge.

In their effort to launch the postponement initiative, when the task force visited the engineering department to ask for the modification of the product, the engineers did not understand why they were being bothered. After all, they had done their job in creating one of the most successful products in *HP* history. Moreover, they did not have any time to allocate to the old product as they were working on the next generation of the Deskjet printer. In any case, this was a materials and information problem: Get the forecast right and have more flexibility in manufacturing, and the problem would be resolved.

When the task force visited the manufacturing site, the reaction was similar. It was not their fault, since they were running a JIT operation. If only they could receive the correct forecasts, they would ship the correct material at the right time. Moreover, one should be careful to do the final quality checks in the field as the company's reputation rode on the performance of its products.

The logistics organization was equally reluctant. Their productivity was measured by the number of orders they filled each day. Under the postponement strategy, they would have to open each box, load the appropriate software, conduct the final tests, repack the product with all the required peripherals, and ship it. This would kill their productivity. If only manufacturing were a bit more agile!

Unfortunately, one cannot blame any of these departments for their reluctance to embrace the postponement strategy. They were given a task and a set of local performance metrics to assess whether they were doing the task properly. As rational decision makers, these departments were indeed optimizing their own operations in a local fashion. They were not required to think about the impact of their local decisions on other stakeholders along the supply chain. They were not incentivized to do so. Why should they incur extra cost or walk the extra mile to make someone else a hero?

To achieve the elusive alignment, SCM involves thinking like an engineer ("people are dumb but honest") with a focus on streamlining processes and educating employees, and like an economist ("people are dishonest but smart") with a focus on implementing the appropriate incentive structures. While a trust-based relationship is always advertised as the ultimate solution, trust has two very concrete dimensions in the SCM context: proof of concept and risks/benefits. Proof of concept is required to establish the capabilities of the parties aiming to construct a collaborative relationship. Risks and benefits represent the quantification of the potential losses and gains, respectively, that each party should expect from such a relationship over and above what exists in a transactional relationship. In short, the challenge is to devise incentive structures that would produce win-win situations.

This was the challenge undertaken by *Barilla* in rolling out a VMI management initiative in Italy with its distributors serving the small independent supermarkets.[2] In a conservative and highly fragmented channel which has traditionally relied on product push strategies through special promotions, discounts, and sales force incentives, the logistics organization of *Barilla* tried to persuade the distributors to adopt VMI. Under the new scheme, instead of placing a replenishment order, the distributor would simply report its own sales data to *Barilla*, which would then automatically provide him with the right replenishment quantities. With its strong brand name and leading market position, *Barilla* never expected any resistance from the distributors, typically small family-owned businesses. Distributors, however, felt quite uncomfortable to report sales data to *Barilla*. They saw in VMI a potential threat of disintermediation in this supply chain.

Some even proposed to sell the sales data to *Barilla*. Others took it personally, telling *Barilla* to manage its own manufacturing operations and leave the distribution to them. They saw no additional economic benefits in the new scheme, but plenty of potential risks for themselves. To add insult to injury, *Barilla*'s own sales force did not believe that the company had the capability to run a VMI program. The rollout collapsed: *Barilla* was all dressed up with nowhere to go.

It was not until *Barilla* generated a proof of concept through pilot runs at its own depots and quantifying the potential benefits and risks of VMI, that distributors started paying attention. According to these early results, the VMI initiative has mitigated the cost-service trade-off through a reduction of up to 50% in inventories concurrently with a significant increase in order fill rates. The distributors were then willing to adopt the VMI initiative once they were presented with some quantification of such risks and benefits.

In fact, the wide success of collaborative initiatives such as ECR and CPFR within the grocery industry is largely based on jointly agreed and adopted voluntary business standards that provide win-win solutions for all the stakeholders, including manufacturers, retailers, logistics service providers, and software vendors.[3] Such practices are quite pragmatic, as in the standardization of pallet sizes (drastically reducing the time trucks wait to be discharged at a retailer's warehouse) or in the adoption of common data definitions and an EDI standard (eliminating the need to duplicate infrastructure investments). Rolling out such initiatives by bringing all the parties on board, however, is still a long process. One therefore needs to construct an objective business case which not only quantifies the potential risks and benefits of such collaborative practices, but also incorporates adequate incentives for all parties to participate in such initiatives.

3.1 A simple framework to quantify the loss

To this end, let us assess the loss incurred in a supply chain in the absence of any collaboration through a simple supply chain model. Consider the following supply chain with a single manufacturer and a single retailer. As depicted in Figure 5.2, a single product is manufactured and sold in the market through the retailer. As a base case, let us assume that this is a vertically integrated setting with both the manufacturer and the retailer belonging to the same firm.

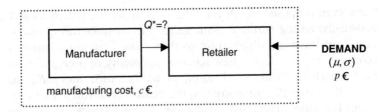

Figure 5.2 An integrated production-distribution system.

The product demand in the market is uncertain. We reflect this uncertainty in our forecast by specifying an average demand level (μ) as well as the volatility of demand expressed by its standard deviation (σ). The product, which incurs a variable manufacturing cost of c €, can be sold in the market for a price of p € (with $p > c$). For the time being, let us ignore the fixed costs; as they will not affect the decision process, we will sweep them under the carpet for now. Once the optimal quantity has been determined, one can then check whether the expected profits are sufficiently high to cover such fixed costs. Given the lead times in the procurement of raw materials and in the production process, the firm has to commit to a certain production level, Q, before observing the actual demand. In other words, the optimal batch size to produce, Q^*, must be determined before the market uncertainty is resolved.

In this setting, the firm is running two types of risks: risk of underage and risk of overage. The *underage risk* is the risk of not producing a sufficient number of units, leading to lost sales, while the *overage risk* is the risk of producing too many units, ending with extra stock at the end of the selling season. The challenge is to produce the lot size that maximizes the expected profit before observing the actual demand.

This problem is so pertinent that it was given a name of its own: the *newsvendor problem*. As a newsvendor, you have to print a certain number of papers the night before so as to sell them the following day. If you print too few copies, you will lose sales; if you print too many copies, you may end up stuck with many unsold newspapers at the end of the day. For simplicity, let us also assume that yesterday's papers are worthless; hence, there is no salvage value. The newsvendor problem applies to all one-shot commitments before the associated uncertainty is resolved. The number of calendars to print for the following year, the amount of raw materials to procure for the upcoming production cycle, the level of capacity to invest in, and type of aircraft (number of seats) to assign to a certain route are all examples of the newsvendor problem.

The following story from the *Straights Times*[4] further illustrates the pertinence of the challenge: "It has been dubbed SS Santa. And some have gone as far as to say Christmas in Europe might have to be cancelled if anything should happen to it. On Saturday, the world's largest ship, the 390m-long *Emma Maersk*, arrived at Felixstowe, Suffolk, and discharged some 3000 containers of Christmas goodies and other products."

With a capacity of 11,000 containers, *Emma Maersk* was delivering on the 4th of November 9,000 pairs of gym shoes, 12,800 MP3 players, 61,800 calendars, 5,170 hand bags, 33,400 cocktail shakers, 11,500 TV sets, and 1,886,000 Christmas decorations, all to be sold during the holiday season. All this merchandise had been ordered and paid for before the demand could be observed. As a result, for some items, the actual demand would surpass the delivered quantity, while for others the unsold items would be deeply discounted in the hope that someone would still buy them after the holidays are over.

Returning to our problem, we need to determine the optimal lot size, Q^*, the one that maximizes the expected profit. We follow a marginal analysis approach to solve the problem. Suppose that you have decided to produce Q units; should you produce one more unit, $Q + 1$? In that case, you have to assess what happens to the additional unit. There are two possibilities: either the additional unit would sell (with the probability that demand exceeds Q units, $Prob\{D > Q\}$) in which case the firm earns a margin of $(p - c)$ € or the additional unit remains unsold (with probability that demand is no more than Q units, $Prob\{D \leq Q\}$) in which case the firm has to absorb the variable manufacturing cost, c €. These outcomes are summarized in the decision tree of Figure 5.3.

The rule of thumb is to continue producing more units as long as the *expected* payoff from that additional unit exceeds the *expected* loss. In other words, continue producing as long as

$$[(p - c) * Prob\{D > Q\}] - [c * Prob\{D \leq Q\}] > 0.$$

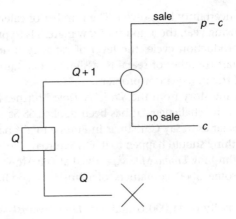

Figure 5.3   Decision tree for the newsvendor problem.

Pushing this rule of thumb to its logical limit tells us to stop as soon as the expected payoff equals the expected loss, which yields the optimal production quantity, Q^*. To obtain the optimal lot size, we note that the above equation reduces to

$$[Prob\{D \le Q\}] = (p - c)/p.$$

Technically, the quantity $(p - c)/p$ represents the critical fractile of the demand distribution, which allows us to compute the optimal lot size, Q^*. For example, if one assumes that the demand process follows a normal distribution with mean, μ, and standard deviation, σ, then the Excel function NORMINV can be used to obtain the optimal quantity:

$$Q^* = \text{NORMINV}[(p - c)/p, \mu, \sigma].$$

Note that the optimal quantity that maximizes the expected profit depends on the average demand, the volatility of the demand, and the financial risk associated with the demand-supply mismatch.

Consider a specific example. Suppose that you would like to bake and sell croissants. You have to get up at 5 a.m. to bake a batch of croissants. Past experience shows that your daily sales are distributed normally with a mean of 500 and a standard deviation of 100.

You can bake a single croissant for 20 cents and sell it for one euro. The question is, therefore, to determine your optimal batch size, i.e., the quantity that maximizes your daily expected profit. Following the above logic, we compute:

$$Q^* = \text{NORMINV}[(1.00 - 0.20)/1.00, 500, 100] = 584.$$

This is the optimal quantity for the entire "production-distribution" system. Let us now embellish our base model shown in Figure 5.2. Suppose that we no longer have a vertically integrated setting, but an independent manufacturer (e.g., a baker) and an independent retailer. The retailer places orders with the manufacturer. The manufacturer produces exactly the quantity ordered by the retailer and delivers it to him, who will later sell them in the market. In other words, the newsvendor problem is solved exclusively by the retailer, who will fully bear the demand-supply mismatch risk. Further note that the retailer does not necessarily know the manufacturer's variable production cost (c €); this is private information. Instead, the retailer knows the wholesale price (w €) published by the manufacturer. The new scenario is summarized in Figure 5.4, where we need to determine the optimal order quantity for the retailer.

The retailer applies the newsvendor logic to solve the problem, as illustrated in Figure 5.5.

The optimal order quantity for the retailer is, therefore, given by

$$Q^* = \text{NORMINV}[(p - w)/p, \mu, \sigma].$$

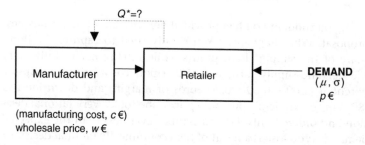

Figure 5.4 A decentralized production-distribution system.

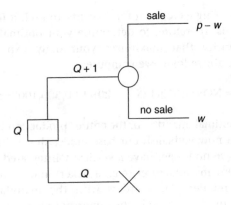

Figure 5.5   Decision tree for the retailer.

Note that the only difference between the two scenarios is the replacement of the variable production cost, c, by the wholesale price, w, in the critical fractile. Returning to our example, suppose that you are too tired after you baked all the croissants at 5 a.m. and that you are looking for someone to sell them for you. You make the following proposal to a friend. She will decide on how many croissants she orders from you based on the available historical data. You will bake those croissants and sell them to her at a wholesale price of 80 cents; she can then sell them on the market for 1 euro each. She therefore needs to determine her optimal order quantity given the market demand and her own demand-supply mismatch risk. Her optimal order quantity is given by:

$$Q^* = \text{NORMINV}[(1.00 - 0.80)/1.00, 500, 100] = 415.$$

Yet you thought you had provided her with an attractive business proposal. What happened? You simply tried to capture the lion's share of the supply chain profits while forcing her to fully carry the demand-supply mismatch risk. Upon considering her upside potential ($1.00 - 0.80 = 0.20$ euros of margin) and downside risk (80 cents of wholesale purchase price), she took a very rational decision and ordered only 415 croissants – even less than the expected demand. Who lost as a result of her economically rational decision? Everyone. In your quest to hijack the supply chain profits, you hurt everyone: the retailer could have sold more, but, given the risk, she chose not to order even the average demand. You, the manufacturer, could have sold more, but did not get the orders. Given that both parties end up getting hurt, we refer to this phenomenon as *double marginalization*. As a result, the entire market pie (i.e., the total value created) got smaller. Note that the customer suffers as well since there will be a higher level of stock-outs in this decentralized setting.

This is the direct consequence of the lack of collaboration in the supply chain: double marginalization, which implies that profits shrink for all involved parties. How can we then restore the profits to the level of a centralized system without having to actually vertically integrate? This is possible only by allowing returns to supply chain partners that are commensurate with the risk they carry.

3.2 Promoting collaboration

While working toward a long-term trust-based relationship, one can design and implement *contractable* incentives. These are incentives that can be observed, verified, and enforced. They include

- Quantity discounts
- Buyback schemes
- Two-part tariffs (selling at cost plus charging a flat fee)
- Profit sharing
- Cost sharing
- Volume guarantees
- Multiyear business guarantees
- Joint-marketing initiatives

These schemes and their variants are easy-to-implement mechanisms to align the divergent priorities of the supply chain partners. For example, offering quantity discounts is equivalent, for a manufacturer, to publishing a matrix of wholesale prices. A buyback scheme is a risk-sharing initiative that enables the retailer to return to the manufacturer unsold units at the end of the selling season. Consider the above example where the manufacturer pledges to accept returns at the end of the season at a buyback price of b €. The resulting scenario is summarized in Figure 5.6 with the corresponding decision tree shown in Figure 5.7. To make the scenario more concrete, suppose that you

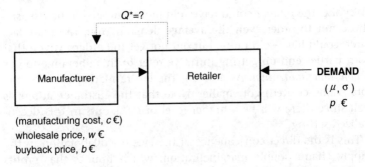

Figure 5.6   A decentralized production-distribution system with buyback.

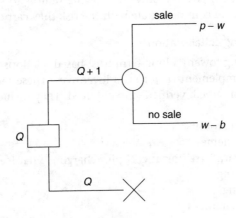

Figure 5.7   Decision tree for the retailer.

agree to buy back the unsold croissants for 50 cents. What is her optimal order quantity under the buyback scheme? The optimal quantity is given by:

$$Q^* = \text{NORMINV}[(p-w)/(p-b), \mu, \sigma].$$

$$Q^* = \text{NORMINV}[0.40, 500, 100] = 475.$$

This is still far from the original (centralized) optimal quantity of 585, but the optimal quantity is moving in the right direction;

coordination is working! This quick calculation shows that a buy-back policy makes perfect mathematical sense. Does it, however, make any business sense? Why would a manufacturer want to buy back his products? There are several business reasons for that. First, it is a strong signal to the retailer that the manufacturer is sharing some of the demand-supply mismatch risk. In so doing, he would be encouraging the retailer to order more, thereby increasing the size of the market pie. Second, the manufacturer may have better alternatives than the retailer for salvaging the unsold units. He may have access to other channels. He may be able to recycle or reman-ufacture the product. Finally, he may not wish the retailer to dis-count the products deeply. A designer would rather take back his stylish handbags than witness the retailer offering deep discounts on them in a desperate attempt to liquidate the leftover stock; that would deeply hurt the designer's image.

One quick way to restore the centralized profits would be for the manufacturer to sell at cost, that is, to set $w = c$. While this would mathematically resolve the issue (i.e., restore the system profit to the original level), it makes no business sense for two reasons. First, in this setting, all the supply chain profits are transferred to (captured by) the retailer. Second, the manufacturer receives nothing, which makes it impossible for him to cover his fixed costs, hence stay in business. One way to get around this problem is to use what econo-mists call a two-part tariff: selling at cost plus imposing a flat fee. Most franchising arrangements follow this practice. Suppose that you operate a hamburger chain. To sell french fries, you purchase a bag of potatoes from the parent company at cost. At the end of the year, however, you write a check, the franchising fee, to the parent company to cover its costs.

Profit sharing may also represent a coordinating contract, as illus-trated by the following example. The second-largest source of revenue for movie studios in the United States turns out to be movie rentals. Hence, once a film completes its primary run in the movie theaters, the studio produces DVDs and sells them to video rental shops. Until a few years ago, such DVDs were priced quite high, making it virtu-ally impossible for the rental shops to make any profit unless they rented the DVD out numerous times. This practice ultimately led to double marginalization. Under the current scheme, the movie studios have drastically cut their sales prices, encouraging the rental shops to order a large number of DVDs to rent out. At the end of the year, however, the studios claim 45% of the rental profits.[5]

These initiatives aim at distributing risks and rewards among the supply chain partners in an equitable fashion. While they are necessary for promoting collaboration, they may not – in and of themselves – be sufficient. Suppose that you are a bicycle manufacturer and you offer your retailer a buyback program. Suppose further that the retailer also carries bicycles from another manufacturer that does not offer buyback. It is the last week of August, the last few days of the selling season. Whose products would you expect the retailer to push for sale? Your competitor's bikes, of course, as you have provided him with a safety net. One should therefore design the incentives carefully. For example, the buyback scheme would kick in once the retailer has achieved a certain sales volume.

4. Collaboration in practice

Collaboration is enabled by sharing information, resources, profits, and risk. Although the ultimate goal in supply chain collaboration is to achieve a win-win proposition for all participating members, there is often a large discrepancy between the potential and the practice. There are no guidelines or standard protocols to manage and control the collaborative efforts of the partners. Trust is an important element in a collaborative relationship but might take a backseat when precedence is given to a company's revenue-making goal. Furthermore, trust cannot be built overnight; it is achieved after a lengthy process of quantifying the risks and the benefits as well as assessing the capabilities of the partners.

While the virtues of collaboration among partners comprising the supply network are constantly promoted in the trade press, in seminars, in textbooks, and in classrooms, there exist very few successful examples of supply chain collaboration. This is in part because collaborative practices are only achieved through explicit and persistent infrastructure investments in design, organizational structures, and technology.

We conducted a survey to identify the current practices and initiatives aimed at creating such an organizational and technological infrastructure to facilitate collaboration among the players in a supply network and assess the costs and benefits of such practices to each of the players.

The survey was composed of six parts:

- Company Characteristics, reflecting the organization's key parameters such as its products, its markets, its size, and its financial performance;
- Supply Chain Design, reflecting the sourcing relationships with the upstream players;
- Channel Management, reflecting the distribution relationships with the downstream players;
- Logistics Management, reflecting the logistics practices within the organization;
- Process Management, reflecting the process characteristics with a view of the organization's operational flexibility;
- Technology Deployment, reflecting the organization's investments and use of infrastructure technologies.

4.1 Company characteristics

The participants in the survey span a wide range of sectors, including

- Agriculture
- Apparel and footwear
- Chemicals
- Consumer electronics
- Eye care
- Fast-moving consumer goods
- IT
- Medical devices
- Precision metal products
- Precision plastic components
- Retail
- Steel making

The annual turnover of the companies in our sample varies from a minimum of 4.47 million euros to a maximum of 3766 million euros. Their cash-to-cash cycle ranges from 14 days minimum to 288 days maximum. The average product life cycle over all the sectors is approximately 12 years, ranging from half a year to 100 years. From a VBM perspective, companies report an average of 12% for ROCE (with a maximum of 23%) or 11.2% for RONA (with a maximum of 20%). The breakdown of supply chain costs as a percentage of total landed cost is presented in Table 5.1.

Table 5.1 Supply chain costs

Supply chain costs	Avg.(%)
• Inbound Logistics	9.3
• Raw Materials and Components	46.2
• Manufacturing and Assembly	30.1
• Warehousing	6.3
• Outbound Logistics	8.1

4.2 Supply chain design

The current supply base management practices are reflected in Table 5.2, where companies report a maximum of 75% of dual sourcing. Companies, on average, certify 45.7% of their suppliers, and only 18.7% of them have developmental programs with them. Joint initiatives account for 25% on average. Only 5% of the suppliers have access to the companies' planning and control system. The average value of all the contract terms also seems to be very low: only 5% of the respondents use VMI, while only 21% receive deliveries on a JIT basis. On average, 15% of the procurement occurs through the Web.

Supplier relations are managed through "traditional" contract terms, including quantity discounts, convenient payment terms, price protection, and multiyear commitments. Policies promoting further alignment such as cost sharing, profit sharing, two-part tariff, or buyback policies are not yet as popular.

4.3 Channel management

Table 5.3 summarizes current practices in the downstream channel. Material flows are mainly triggered through a direct order by channel partners; only a very small percentage is attributable to continuous replenishment, short-term forecasts. There is no joint forecast in this case. On average, 35% of deliveries are done on a JIT basis; VMI is used only by 7% of the respondents.

Only 10.3% of the channel partners have access to the planning and control system of their partners. 19.5% of the companies report joint marketing initiatives. Quantity discounts seem to be the most favored policy along with convenient payment terms.

In addition to traditional contract terms such as quantity discounts, convenient payment terms, multiyear or volume guarantees,

Table 5.2 Characteristics of the supply base

Sourcing	Min. (%)	Avg. (%)	Max. (%)
Single	0	57	100
Dual	0	25	75
Certification (Avg.)		45.7	
Devl. Prog.	0	18	90
Joint Initiatives	0	25	100
Order triggers			
• direct order	15	48	100
• continuous replenishment	0	48	60
• short-term forecast	0	48	70
• customer's orders	0	40	60
• joint forecast	0	30	37
• other	0	2.5	25
Access to planning	0	14	100
VMI	0	5	30
Contract terms			
• Quantity discounts	0	34	100
• Convenient payment terms	0	43	90
• Price protection	0	41	100
• Consignment stocks	0	2	10
• Buyback policies	0	1	20
• Profit sharing	0	0	5
• Cost sharing	0	5	50
• Two-part tariff (at cost + flat fee)	0	4	30
• Volume guarantees	0	14	100
• Multiyear commitment	0	23	100
• Other	0	1	10

more progressive alignment policies such as buyback, consignment or cost sharing have started taking root in the relationships with the channel members.

4.4 Logistics management

From Table 5.4, it can be seen that all the companies use external logistics providers for outbound transportation whereas 80% of the companies use them for inbound transportation as well. However, none of the companies use the external services providers for order entry and customer services, making sure that direct customer contact

Table 5.3 Channel relationships

Channel	Min. (%)	Avg. (%)	Max. (%)
Order triggers			
• their direct order	0	75	100
• continuous replenishment	0	11	80
• their short-term forecast	0	7	50
• their customer's orders	0	6	50
• joint forecast	0	1	10
• other	0	0	0
Access to planning	0	6.3	100
Joint marketing	0	19.5	60
Post-sales support	0	38.6	100
Contract terms			
• Quantity discounts	0	40.3	100
• Convenient payment terms	0	41	100
• Price protection	0	21.8	100
• Consignment stocks	0	11.4	75
• Buyback policies	0	13.5	90
• Profit sharing	0	1.5	20
• Cost sharing	0	10	80
• Two-part tariff (at cost + flat fee)	0	1	10
• Volume guarantees	0	23.3	100
• Multiyear commitment	0	21.4	100
• Other	0	2	20

is not lost. Most of the companies have "cost sharing" relationships with their partners.

4.5 Process management

Table 5.5 summarizes some key process characteristics. Production schedules are revised at least once a month and at most every day of the month. Average Customer Order Lead Time is approximately 9 days. The average inventory level for the raw materials is the highest with approximately 18 days while that for the WIP is 9 days and for the finished goods is 12.5 days.

The on-time-in-full delivery performance is on average 91% with a maximum of 99.96%, while fill rates hover around 84% with a maximum of 100%. The cash-to-cash cycle is 89 days on average with a minimum of 14 days and a maximum of 228 days.

Table 5.4 Logistics services

Logistics	% Usage
External services used	
• Warehousing	30
• Outbound Transportation	100
• Freight Bill Auditing/Payment	30
• Inbound Transportation	80
• Freight Consolidation and Distribution	40
• Cross Docking	30
• Product Marking, Labeling, and Packaging	40
• Selected Manufacturing Activities	40
• Product Returns/Repair	30
• Inventory Management	10
• Traffic Management/Fleet Operations	40
• IT	20
• Product Assembly/Installation	10
• Order Fulfilment	10
• Order Entry/Order Processing	0
• Customer Service (after-sales service, warranty management, spare parts management, etc.)	0
Contract type	
• Joint Venture	0
• Revenue Sharing	10
• Gain Sharing	0
• Cost Sharing	60
• Risk Sharing	20

Table 5.5 Process characteristics

Process	Min.	Avg.	Max.
Prod. Sched.Change	1		30
Lead Time (in days)	1	9.2	30
On-Time-In-Full Delivery (%)		91	99.96
Fill Rate (%)		84	100
Cash-to-Cash Cycle (in days)	14	89	228
Inv. Coverage (in days)			
• raw materials	4.4	17.7	56
• work-in-process	4.4	9.1	20
• finished goods	3.4	12.54	25

Table 5.6 Total IT spend

IT	Min. (%)	Avg. (%)	Max. (%)
IT SPEND	0.40	1.85	4.00

Table 5.7 IT deployed

Technology	% Deployed
EDI	70
ERP	90
Supply Chain Planning	70
E-Procurement	60
CRM	40
Web Services	80

4.6 Information technology

SCM is an information-intensive process. It is therefore natural that companies in our sample invest up to 4% of their annual sales in IT (See Table 5.6).

On the software side, the emphasis has shifted on planning tools as well as on more advanced Web-based technologies once the Y2K craze had blown over. The percentage of companies that deploy the different IT solutions is as shown in Table 5.7. These systems are used by 17–54% of the total workforce.

5. Summary

- The key challenge in modern supply chains is the coordination of the players in the ecosystem without the presence of a clear command and control structure. The lack of coordination contributes to the bullwhip phenomenon driven by delays and distortions in material and information flows, respectively.
- Good SCM involves thinking like an engineer ("people are dumb but honest") with a focus on streamlining processes and educating employees, and like an economist ("people are dishonest but smart") with a focus on implementing the appropriate incentive structures. While a trust-based relationship is always advertised as the ultimate solution, the challenge is to devise incentive structures that would produce win-win situations.
- The deployment of such incentives remains limited.

6

Impact of Technology on SCM

1. Introduction

The 1986 Annual Report of the *Digital Equipment Corporation (DEC)* was setting an ambitious goal:

> "Our goal is to connect all parts of an organization – the office, the factory floor, the laboratory, the engineering department – from desktop to data center. We can connect everything within a building; we can connect a group of buildings on the same site or at remote sites; we can connect an entire organization around the world. We propose to connect a company from top to bottom with a single network that includes the shipping clerk, the secretary, the manager, the vice president, even the president."[1]

More importantly, this goal was based not on some "vaporware" but on a concrete enabling technology, namely a new generation of super minicomputers based on a single computer architecture, VAX. From small desktop machines to computer clusters, VAX-based machines would be fully compatible, use a uniform operating system, and communicate across shared networks.

While *DEC* was working on the hardware, the operating system, and the infrastructure, a relatively young German company, *SAP AG*, was taking on a big gamble by transitioning its mainframe-based ERP software, the R/2, into the client-server architecture, the R/3, making the software accessible to thousands of organizations that did not necessarily want to invest in mainframe computers.

However, it took almost two decades – during which computing power has tremendously increased and the Internet has become ubiquitous – for *DEC*'s 1986 vision of creating a networked organization to become a reality. In fact, scholars of strategic management increasingly recognize that the source of value creation may lie in networks of firms (Dyer and Nobeoka 2000, Gulati et al. 2000). Amit and Zott (2001) further build on this line of thinking by suggesting that value is created by the way in which transactions are enabled. Enabling such transactions requires a network of capabilities drawn from multiple stakeholders, such as customers, suppliers, and complementors.

Information plays a crucial role in enabling transactions in supply chains. Creating an adequate information infrastructure to interface the members of a supply network has always been challenging. Such an infrastructure must be able to satisfy *simultaneously* the following needs (Upton and McAfee 1996): first, it must be able to accommodate members with varying degrees of IT sophistication. Second, it must provide a wide range of functionality ranging from simple data transmission to capability of accessing remote applications. Finally, it must be able to accommodate a constantly changing ecosystem of suppliers and customers within varying stages of relationships.

In a recent workshop, supply chain professionals highlighted four shortcomings in current ERP systems (Akkermans et al. 2003): (1) extended enterprise (EE) functionality, (2) flexibility in adapting to changes in the environment, (3) more advanced decision support functionality, and (4) lack of (Web-enabled) modularity. While Web-based technologies enable the management of a portfolio of relationships in an effective and efficient manner by drastically reducing transaction costs, the cost of establishing such relationships remains. Furthermore, while the developments in the computing and telecommunications industries made the transfer of information almost instantaneous, manufacturing, warehousing, and distribution technologies could not accelerate the movement of material to such phenomenal levels. The coordination of information, cash, and material flows has thus assumed an increased importance for effective SCM.

The transition from the mainframe to the client-server architecture was the key technological breakthrough that unleashed the first ERP revolution. The adoption of SOA holds the promise of triggering the second wave by enabling the dynamic reconfiguration of supply chains, making them readily adaptable to changing business models, growing competition and globalization, tighter regulations, and increased mergers and acquisition activities.

The enabling technology is Web services. A Web service is a self-contained, self-describing piece of application functionality that can be found and accessed by other applications using open standards. By using highly standardized interfaces to hide the implementation of the underlying functionality, Web services enable interoperability and compatibility among various heterogeneous applications. In fact, ERP vendors are extending Web services standards and SOA principles to develop composite applications to support new business processes or scenarios. For example, *SAP*'s *Enterprise Services Architecture* (ESA) aggregates Web services into business-level enterprise services, providing more meaningful building blocks for the task of dynamically adapting the IT infrastructure to evolving business conditions.

In this chapter, we review the impact of the ERP revolution, the Internet, and other Web-based technologies on supply chain strategies. While the impact of IT on supply chain coordination has been undeniably positive, some reservations remain regarding its impact on supply chain design. The remainder of the chapter is organized as follows: Section 2 briefly introduces key trends in SCM. Section 3 illustrates the role of IT in SCM and IT's ability in keeping up with these trends. Section 4 discusses the challenges of dynamic supply chain design. Section 5 concludes the chapter with practical guidelines.

2. Key trends in SCM

Akkermans et al. (2003) report a ranked list of key SCM trends generated by a group of European SCM professionals. As summarized in Table 6.1, the panel of experts sees further integration of activities between suppliers and customers across the entire chain as one of the three biggest trends in SCM. This view coincides with a strong trend toward mass customization. Both trends may have a similar root cause, i.e., increased competition driven by growing consumer power helped by an increasing transparency of the global market place. Rapidly changing customer requirements not only tolerate very little inventory in the supply chain, but also require drastic modifications in supply chain topologies. This requirement poses a tough challenge

Table 6.1 Key trends in SCM (Top-12 of 22)

Key issues in SCM	Votes (%)
1. Further integration of activities between suppliers and customers across the entire chain	87
2. How to maintain flexibility in ERP systems to deal with changing supply chain needs?	57
3. Mass customization: complex assortments, shorter cycle times, and less inventory	39
4. Who will be in the driver's seat in supply chain coordination?	35
5. Supply chains consisting of several enterprises	35
6. Full exchange of information with all the players in the chain	35
7. Further outsourcing of activities such as physical distribution, F & A	30
8. Enhancements of IT tools required to integrate the different parties in the supply chain	30
9. Globalization: how to build worldwide ERP systems?	26
10. Greater transparency of the global market place	26
11. Internet technology will be the backbone to connect systems of partners in the chain	26
12. Standardization of processes and information definitions, the rest is IT infrastructure	22

to ERP systems for maintaining sufficient flexibility as supply chain needs keep evolving.

SCM experts recognize that it is difficult for a single organization to satisfy the changing requirements of consumers. They expect that supply chains will consist of several enterprises and that noncore activities such as physical distribution and Finance and Administration (F&A) will be increasingly outsourced. An important issue for the panel, then, becomes the determination of who will be sitting in the "driver's seat" in this chain, since conventional command-and-control structures no longer apply in a network of independent firms.

Greater and faster-changing demands from customers will need to lead to faster and more comprehensive information exchanges among all the players in the chain. In terms of technology, this will not just mean better ERP systems but, in general, enhanced IT tools to integrate the different parties in the supply chain. Internet technology is most likely to provide the technological means for doing so. This will make distributed architectures, in which standardization takes place mainly at the level of information definitions and processes, possible so that local flexibility in information usage can be maintained. Needless to say, all these developments are taking place on a global scale. Hence, IT for SCM in general, and ERP systems in particular, will have to be developed on a global basis.

3. IT in supply chain coordination

Information is said to be the glue that holds supply chains together. In fact, the bullwhip phenomenon, the key challenge in supply chain coordination, is driven by delayed and distorted information as well as by transaction costs promoting local optimization (Lee et al. 1997). ITs have the greatest impact on supply chain coordination through the elimination of information delays and distortions, and through the reduction of transaction costs.

As indicated in the previous section, creating an adequate information infrastructure to interface the members of a supply chain has always been challenging. According to Upton and McAfee (1996), such an infrastructure must be able to satisfy *simultaneously* the following needs: first, it must be able to accommodate members with varying degrees of IT sophistication. Second, it must provide a wide range of functionality ranging from simple data transmission to access for remote applications. Finally, it must be able to accommodate a constantly changing pool of suppliers and customers within varying stages of relationships.

Figure 6.1 depicts these three dimensions of *electronic connectivity*. The utility of potential infrastructure technologies can then be assessed by how well these technologies "fill the cube." For example, EDI has been the most widely used tool for connecting players in a supply chain such as manufacturers and their suppliers. From a functionality perspective, EDI affords simple data transmission under a particular file format over a dedicated communication channel. Rudimentary computer skills are required for maintaining EDI connectivity. Given the dedicated communications infrastructure and the proprietary standards, however, EDI necessitates significant up-front investment and considerable expense for maintenance. Such an investment is difficult to justify at the early stages of a buyer-supplier relation, where the buyer is in the process of assessing

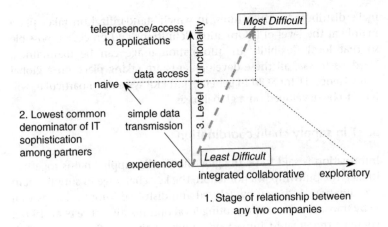

Figure 6.1   Upton and McAfee's framework for electronic connectivity.

supplier capability and, therefore, is unwilling to provide any long-term commitment.

Groupware extends the limited information transmission func tionality of EDI into a (limited) collaborative platform. However, the required computer skills to take full advantage of groupware's capabilities are even higher than the skills required to use EDI. Furthermore, groupware requires even a higher initial investment than EDI, which, once again, makes the tool more appropriate at more advanced stages of a supply chain relationship. One can obtain further IT functionality by establishing a wide-area network. Such a platform can be used not only for information transmission, but also for collaboration and granting access to application programs, i.e., telepresence, for the suppliers. Unfortunately, the increased functionality comes at a higher level of initial investment. One can also envisage such an infrastructure only among close partners along the supply chain. In summary, traditional technologies always entail a trade-off: improvements in one dimension (e.g., enhanced functionality) come at the expense of further complications in at least one of the other two dimensions (e.g., higher initial investments).

ERP systems, which arguably had the most significant impact on SCM, could not initially break this trade-off. On the functionality dimension, ERP systems offer the opportunity for unparalleled transparency across the organization, making a single database visible for all the (at least, internal) stakeholders. This visibility may, in turn, enable closer cooperation. These capabilities, however, can only be deployed through long and expensive implementation processes, which typically require advanced levels of IT sophistication. Furthermore, best-practice templates that often guide ERP implementations limit the scope of applicability of these systems to advanced stages of relationships among collaborating organizations. In short, ERP systems fail to fully "fill the cube" as well. This failure is discussed in further depth in the next section.

3.1 SCM shortcomings of current ERP systems

Akkermans et al. (2003) report that industry experts highlighted four key shortcomings in ERP. These shortcomings are listed in Table 6.2 along with a pointer to the key SCM trends summarized in Table 6.1.

Lack of EE functionality

Extended enterprise functionality entails the ability to share internal data efficiently with supply chain partners and to accommodate the data made available by the partners. Data sharing can be deployed either for operational decision making or for calculating supply chain–wide performance measures. Moreover, EE functionality enables business processes to be distributed over multiple organizational entities. For instance, in a classical order-capturing process, this would mean doing a distributed available-to-promise (ATP) check, delegating the credit check to a financial service provider, and relying on a logistic service provider to be able to promise a specific delivery time window.

Lack of flexibility in adapting to changing supply chain needs

A single organization might have different types of relationships with its supplier and customer base. Its ERP system should be sufficiently flexible to accommodate a multitude of relationships. Some suppliers may have adopted VMI while others may still be engaged in a classical vendor/buyer relation. The ERP system should be able to accommodate all these different modes of collaboration simultaneously and be able to change efficiently from one mode to another. Gartner Institute emphasizes that the ability to engage in – and disengage from – collaborative relationships is of critical importance.

Table 6.2   Shortcomings of current ERP systems for SCM

Shortcomings of current ERP systems mentioned, grouped by common threads	Key SCM Trends from Table 6.1
1. Lack of EE functionality: the ability to support operations across multiple organizations	
• EE functionality	1. (Integration)
• EE functionality	4. (Driver seat)
• ERP systems miss linking across the boundaries of enterprises	7. (Transparency)
• ERP systems do not interconnect easily with other than partner systems	7. (Transparency)
• Information exchange between parties is underdeveloped	1. (Integration)
• Ability to support multiple coding system to enable cross-company implementations	1. (Integration)
2. Lack of flexibility in adapting to ever-changing supply chain needs	
• Flexibility to adapt to changing business models	3. (Customization)
• Flexibility to adapt to changes in business processes	7. (Transparency)
3. Lack of more advanced supporting functionality beyond transaction management	
• Flow-based information exchange instead of ordering-based	1. (Integration)
• MRP-based instead of finite capacity; ERP+ required	1. (Integration)
• Advanced planning systems with proven functionality	3. (Customization)
• Connections with tactical decisions	4. (Driver seat)
• From transactions to information for decision-support	4. (Driver seat)
4. Lack of open, modular, Internet-like system architectures	
• Modular set of systems	4. (Driver seat)
• Module manager for the supply chain	4. (Driver seat)
• Connectivity	3. (Customization)
• Web-enabled ERP	6. (Information exchange)
5. Various	
• IT (network technology; big, shared databases; XML,etc.)	6. (Information exchange)
• Customization will remain necessary	1. (Integration)
• Identification of barriers and developing business cases to overcome these	6. (Information exchange)

Another type of flexibility is the possibility of redesigning business processes. Supply chain design is facilitated not only by a set of enabling ITs, but also by a set of new and/or redesigned processes. On the one hand, IT cannot enhance supply chain performance unless processes and organizational structures are redesigned. On the other hand, process reengineering relies heavily on the use of IT to create innovative processes for enhancing supply chain performance. Here ERP offers indeed a considerable opportunity: when implementing an ERP system, which will change the way people work, it seems logical to combine this effort with BPR along the supply chain.

Lack of advanced decision support capabilities

A recent trend in ERP is the emergence of Advanced Planning and Scheduling systems (APS). In itself, planning with longer time horizons and across different business units is nothing new for ERP. However, as it becomes increasingly apparent that supply chains, rather than individual organizations, compete, there is an increasing demand for collaborative architectures in decision-support software.

Lack of open, modular system architecture

Current ERP systems lack a modular, open, and Internet-like system architecture. Basically, this shortcoming is the reverse side of some of the generic advantages of ERP, whereby ERP was originally intended to replace a multitude of local legacy systems; a great deal of emphasis was, therefore, placed on its integrated architecture. In the new, networked economy, this former strength has rapidly become a weakness.

3.2 Web services and SOA

The incorporation of Web-based technologies into ERP systems not only addresses these shortcomings, but also eliminates the electronic connectivity trade-off in Figure 6.1. Transmission Control Protocol/Internet Protocol (TCP/IP) provides a universal communication standard over the Internet for connecting diverse computer systems. A universal communication standard, in turn, significantly reduces the up-front investment needed to connect various players along the supply chain regardless of the type of hardware they possess. Low entry and exit costs make the Internet and Web-based applications affordable at any stage of a supply chain relationship. Given the flexibility to customize the interface over the Web, one can customize the communication channels for each supplier. Web-based technologies also provide a full portfolio of functionality ranging from simple information transmission to telepresence. Standardized interfaces and application development software make it easy even for the uninitiated to start using the system quickly, further reducing the lowest common denominator of IT sophistication among the supply chain entities.

In short, Web-based technologies *fill the cube*. Wider acceptance of open standards, cheap and powerful computing, increased bandwidth, enhanced security, and accumulated expertise and higher familiarity with the technology are bound to increase the utility of Web-based technologies in supply chain coordination. With increased connectivity, the Web provides a virtually free platform for enhancing transparency, eliminating information delays and distortions, and reducing transaction costs, ultimately mitigating the bullwhip phenomenon.

The transition from the mainframe to the client-server architecture was the key technological breakthrough that unleashed the first ERP revolution. The adoption of Web services and the SOA holds the promise of unleashing the second wave by enabling the dynamic reconfiguration of supply chains. The enabling technology is Web services, which denote a group of technologies that allow business processes or information to be accessed over the Internet through application-to-application interaction (Moitra and Ganesh 2005). Web services are loosely coupled, dynamically bound, accessible over the Web, and standards based. In fact, the World Wide Web Consortium (W3C) Architecture Working Group defines Web services as "software applications identified by a Universal Resource Indicator, whose interfaces and bindings are capable of being defined, described, and discovered as XML artifacts." In layman's terms, Web services can be published, located, and invoked by other applications over the Internet, thereby integrating applications written in different languages and operating on disparate platforms.

A Web service is thus a self-contained, self-describing piece of application functionality that can be found and accessed by other applications using open standards. A Web service is self-contained in that the application using the Web service does not have to depend on anything other than the service itself. It is self-describing in that all the information on how to use the service can be obtained from the service itself. The descriptions are centrally stored and accessible through Web-standards-based mechanisms to all applications that wish to invoke the service. By using highly standardized interfaces to hide the implementation of the underlying functionality, Web services enable interoperability and compatibility among various heterogeneous applications.

Web services make available open and standardized interfaces, allowing for the encapsulation and the componentization of software and applications. Hence, they enable easy configuration and reconfiguration of software applications. In other words, instead of requiring programmers to establish and maintain links between applications, Web services are loosely coupled, enhancing flexibility and promoting reuse. Changes can be made in the underlying implementation or in the program calling the Web service as long as the behavior of the Web service stays the same.

The underlying philosophy behind Web services is based on SOA. It would allow service providers (such as ERP vendors and their complementors) to publish services, which may be accessed by the service consumers (such as members of a supply network) resulting in a high degree of service reuse.

Consider, for example, the functionality "delete order" that may necessitate cross-application activities, including sending a confirmation to the customer, removing the order from the production plan, releasing materials allocated to the order, notifying the invoicing department, and changing the order status and deleting it from various systems. Instead of the hard wiring illustrated in Figure 6.2, each of these activities may be a Web service offered by different systems. The ability to build a complex end-to-end solution to cancel an order would be a powerful enterprise-level business service. Web services, however, are too granular to be used as efficient building blocks for enterprise business scenarios. In fact, ERP vendors are extending Web services standards and SOA principles to develop composite applications to support new business processes or scenarios. *SAP's* ESA, built on its *NetWeaver* platform, is illustrated in Figure 6.3. Aggregating Web services into business-level enterprise services provides more meaningful building blocks for the task of dynamically adapting the IT infrastructure to evolving business conditions.

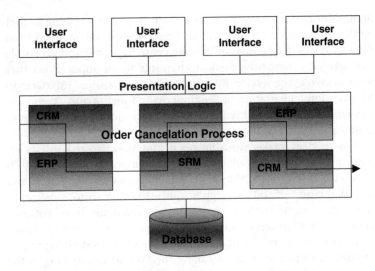

Figure 6.2   Canceling an order in the three-tier client-server architecture.

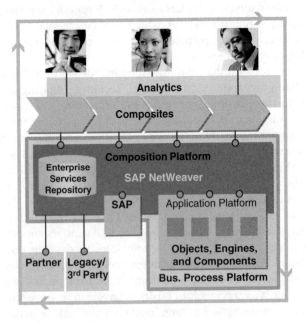

Figure 6.3   SAP's ESA.

4. IT in supply chain design

The impact of Web-based technologies is less convincing for supply chain design. A novel framework for dynamically guiding supply chain design is 3D-CE. As introduced by Fine (1998), 3D-CE encourages the simultaneous design of products, processes, and supply chains and explicitly considers the interfaces among these three dimensions. Some of these interfaces are well understood. Design for x (DFx) (where x can denote design for manufacturability in DFM or design for localization in DFL) captures the interdependence of product and process design decisions (Stoll 1986). Similarly, the interface between product and supply chain design is well understood by trying to match agile supply chains with innovative products and efficient supply chains with functional products (Fisher 1997). One of the key, but less well understood, interfaces in 3D-CE is between process design and supply chain design, where the principal decision is what to produce in-house and what to outsource. The outsourcing decision, which is based on a company's competitive capabilities, is thus based on a company's needs for additional manufacturing capacity or for external capability (and/or technology). While toy manufacturers like *Mattel* rely on outsourcing for additional capacity, equipment manufacturers may rely on suppliers for tight-tolerance machining.

To appreciate the impact of Web-based technologies on the make-vs-buy decisions, hence, on the procurement process, consider Forrester's business-to-business (B2B) digital transaction models reproduced in Figure 6.4. Web-based technologies enable different formats of relationships among potential buyers and vendors. This is indeed consistent with our earlier assessment that the Web provides a platform that simultaneously satisfies all three dimensions of the electronic connectivity requirements (Figure 6.1), including the stage of relationship between any two companies, the lowest common denominator of IT sophistication among partners, and the desired level of functionality.

At the one-to-one level, the Web provides a platform for electronic collaboration, as exemplified by the relationships between *Cisco* and its suppliers. Web-based technologies also offer alternative transaction models for one-to-many and many-to-many environments. In fact, the real power of the Web-based technologies is in their ability to bring together a large number of buyers and sellers in fragmented markets, creating electronic marketplaces. Malone et al. (1987)

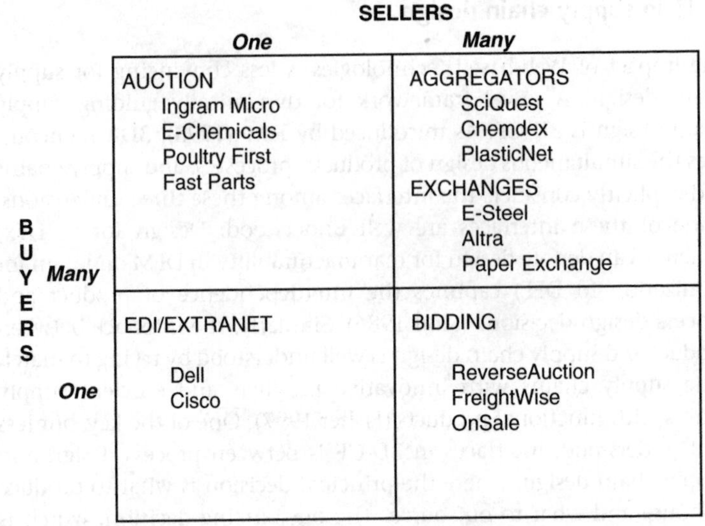

		SELLERS	
		One	*Many*

B **U** **Y** **E** **R** **S** *Many*		AUCTION
		  Ingram Micro
		  E-Chemicals
		  Poultry First
		  Fast Parts
			AGGREGATORS
			  SciQuest
			  Chemdex
			  PlasticNet
			EXCHANGES
			  E-Steel
			  Altra
			  Paper Exchange

One		EDI/EXTRANET
		
		  Dell
		  Cisco
			BIDDING
			
			  ReverseAuction
			  FreightWise
			  OnSale

Figure 6.4   Business-to-business digital transaction models.

broadly define e-markets as IT-based governance or coordination mechanisms. According to *Jupiter Communications*, in 2004, e-markets produced an online transaction volume of $6 billion in the United States. Based on transaction theory, Malone et al. (1987) suggest that IT reduces transaction and coordination costs and will, therefore, lead to an overall shift from hierarchical coordination to market coordination. In fact, total savings in Web-based procurement can reach 13–28%. Most of these savings come from reduced costs of search (need identification 11%, vendor selection 27%, vendor approval 23%) and of coordination (order processing, billing, and payment processing 18%; tracking and logistics administration 21%).

E-markets then pose a dilemma for buyers and vendors. Most manufacturers spent the past two decades establishing close relationships with their suppliers under such different initiatives as strategic sourcing and supply-base rationalization. E-markets, on the other hand, signal a dramatic shift toward an arm's length relationship focusing solely on cost reduction. Within this shift, the promised transaction cost reductions associated with vendor selection and vendor approval necessitate closer scrutiny.

	Operating Inputs	Manufacturing Inputs
Systematic Sourcing	**MRO HUBS** www.grainger.com www.mro.com	**CATALOG HUBS** www.chemconnect.com www.plasticsnet.com
Spot Sourcing	**YIELD MANAGERS** www.employease.com www.capacityweb.com	**EXCHANGES** www.e-steel.com www.paperexchange.com

Figure 6.5   Kaplan and Shawney's B2B trading matrix.

From this perspective, the items purchased by a manufacturer can be classified in two broad categories: manufacturing inputs, goods that go directly into a product or a process, and operating inputs, usually referred to as MRO. While manufacturing inputs vary widely from industry to industry and are hence purchased from industry-specific suppliers, MRO is not necessarily industry specific and can, therefore, be purchased from vendors serving many industries. Similarly, procurement practices can be classified under two broad categories: systematic sourcing, where long-term contracts are negotiated with prequalified suppliers; and spot sourcing, where an immediate need is fulfilled at the lowest possible cost perhaps from anonymous parties. Putting these two dimensions of what to purchase and how to purchase it on a B2B matrix (Figure 6.5) offers some interesting insights (Kaplan and Shawney 2000).

W.W. Grainger is a distributor of MRO supplies in the United States, offering over 200,000 products ranging from nuts and bolts to machine lubricants through its website. Such websites can be further extended into hubs with multiple suppliers greatly expanding the number of items offered. MRO hubs constitute an example where the Internet is ideally suited for eliminating the inefficiencies of the current channel by lowering transaction costs, by integrating lower-tier suppliers, by eliminating the duplication of data entry, and by expanding the product portfolio.

MRO procurement can be further extended by yield managers. While buyers are seeking further cost reductions, e-markets are providing the necessary IT infrastructure for conducting on-line auctions. For example, *FreeMarkets* has conducted some 30 "competitive bidding events" (CBE) for *United Technologies* (*UTC*) in 1999 totaling just under

$250 million of purchase volume. *UTC* reports cost reductions of 10–70% in such diverse categories as rivets and studs, logistics services, telephone services, and tax preparation.

For manufacturing inputs, e-markets provide two key benefits. First, catalog hubs offer the possibility of bringing together a virtually unlimited number of offers from different suppliers on a global scale. Such an infrastructure would greatly reduce the search cost for the buyer. For the supplier – in particular, for the small supplier – the platform offers unparalleled access to potential buyers. This is indeed the first step in systematic sourcing. As for spot sourcing, Web-based technologies provide, for the first time, yield management capabilities for manufactured products. A manufacturer stuck with low capacity utilization in a particular month can bid for orders to fill up its fixed production capacity or a buyer with an unexpected shortage of a manufacturing input can bid for the material available on the market in the same way as airlines price their seats or hotels price their rooms (McAfee and McMillan 1987).

Unlike MRO procurement, however, manufacturing inputs are industry specific, where longer-term contracts are negotiated with specific, typically prequalified, suppliers. In this domain, the procurement process is typically divided into three stages: strategic sourcing, supplier management, and day-to-day purchasing. Strategic sourcing includes supplier identification, certification, and selection. Supplier management is concerned with supplier integration, supplier performance evaluation, and contract management. Beyond these two stages we find the day-to-day purchasing activities, including order request, logistics coordination, and payment management. There is no doubt that Web-based technologies drastically reduce day-to-day purchasing costs. Our hesitation, therefore, concentrates on the first two stages of the procurement process. While e-markets provide support for request-for-information (RFI) or request-for-quote (RFQ) preparation, supplier performance evaluation, and contract management, the crucial activity of supplier identification and certification is still affected by the richness/reach trade-off (Evans and Wurster 1999). *Reach* refers to the number of people and products that are accessible quickly and cheaply in virtual markets; *richness* refers to the depth and detail of information that can be accumulated, offered, and exchanged among market participants.

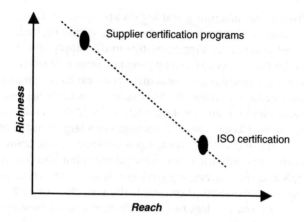

Figure 6.6 Reach vs richness trade-off in supplier certification.

For supplier selection and certification, the trade-off is depicted in Figure 6.6. During the quality movement of the past two decades, a large number of companies have undergone the ISO certification process. As a result, in RFIs or RFQs, ISO certification has become a natural requirement. The certification, therefore, has achieved worldwide recognition, resulting in great reach. Many buyers, however, have quickly discovered that ISO certification is a necessary *but not sufficient* assessment of a potential supplier's process capability. In the automotive and aerospace industries, in particular, manufacturers launched their own certification processes ensuring critical process capability at potential suppliers. While these supplier certification programs possess the desired richness, they have limited reach due to their intensive resource requirements. In most cases, companies have been devising multiyear strategic sourcing programs to reduce and certify their supply base.

While Web-based technologies greatly increase the reach, it is not evident whether they are currently providing the necessary richness for effective supplier selection – hence, the configuration of the supply chain. We observe two approaches to mitigate this trade-off. The first, the market-making process, relies heavily on preliminary fieldwork to identify, assess, and certify suppliers prior to inviting them to join the CBE. There is also considerable effort in defining the "lots" for bidding to create a bundle of products and/or services that make sense from a manufacturing and logistics perspective. Hence, market makers, owners of e-markets, are becoming certifying bodies in the supplier selection process (or navigators in the supply space) with the same credibility challenge faced by previous certifying bodies. A second approach is the creation of vertical markets (or exchanges) managed by industry-specific professionals. Alternatively, incumbents opening a Web-based channel do not face such a credibility challenge. For example, while *ChemConnect* brings together a large number of manufacturers in the chemical sector, *Chemsinglesource.com,* launched by *Solvay,* offers not only the commodity products but also the specialty chemicals and the engineering services offered by the company. The challenge for incumbents, however, is the scalability of such a channel (or reach) and the logistics infrastructure needed to support the virtual channel.

While necessary, technology is thus not sufficient in and of itself for dynamic supply chain design. Many researchers have suggested that it is not sufficient that Web-based technologies and e-markets provide the potential for higher transaction volumes, lower transaction costs, and better market mediation. Other factors such as transaction complexity and frequency, decision powers, existing market structure, and incomplete contracts may impact the formation and sustainability of markets or hierarchies (Wang and Benaroch 2004).

However, one big challenge remains. The shift from hierarchical coordination to market coordination replaces industry structures dominated by vertical integration with networked organizations or loosely coupled ecosystems. In the absence of a clear command-and-control structure, coordination among the members of a supply chain is not trivial, necessitating the implementation of incentive schemes for aligning the divergent economic interests of the members (Tsay et al. 1999). To render electronic markets attractive and sustainable, Wang and Benaroch (2004) propose not only coordination of contracts between buyers and vendors, but also economic incentives to encourage supplier participation in the form of a cap on the transaction fees imposed by the market maker and/or the payment of a premium by the buyer.

Similarly, Bailey and Bakos (1997) suggest four particular roles for electronic intermediaries: facilitation of transactions, trust building to prevent opportunistic behavior, matching of buyers and sellers, and aggregation of supply and demand. Others propose additional new roles such as designing innovative procurement practices and providing novel types of transactions. Such innovative procurement practices and novel types of transactions should, therefore, include contractible initiatives (e.g., buyback policies, quantity flexibility, price protection, and options contracts as discussed in Chapter 5) to ensure that Pareto improves supply chain designs by aligning the economic incentives of buyers and suppliers.

5. Summary

Web-based technologies have a significant impact on supply chain strategies. Swaminathan and Tayur (2003) provide an overview of analytical research models developed to address critical issues such as procurement and supplier management, visibility and information sharing, pricing and distribution, customization and postponement, and enterprise software and real-time decision technologies within the context of e-business. Sodhi (2001) emphasizes the opportunity to further improve planning and execution by extending the decision horizon for planning within the enterprise; by broadening the physical scope beyond the enterprise to customers and suppliers; and by expanding the functional scope to include product design, marketing, and customer relationship management through the deployment of operations research techniques in Web-enabled supply chains.

On the coordination side, the Web provides a virtually free platform for enhancing transparency, eliminating information delays and distortions, and significantly reducing transaction costs. As a result, the Web makes it easier to mitigate the bullwhip phenomenon. On the design side, current technology does not yet permit the mitigation of the trade-off between richness and reach in the crucial task of dynamically reconfiguring the IT infrastructure. The deployment of Web services and SOA principles constitutes a big step toward dynamic supply chain design by enabling the IT infrastructure to evolve with the changing business conditions, making them readily adaptable to changing business models, growing competition and globalization, tighter regulations, and increased mergers and acquisition activities.

More technology (i.e., higher levels of technology adoption), however, should not automatically be equated to higher business performance. In a study of the adoption of the Quick Response (QR) program in the specialty retailing industry, Palmer and Markus (2000) find an association between adoption of QR (at a minimal level) and firm performance, and a high-level alignment between the IT adopted and strategic goals. However, they could not find any support for the hypothesis that higher levels of QR adoption lead to higher business performance, or that poor IT fit with strategy leads to poorer performance. The conclusion should, therefore, not be "more" technology, but "adequate" technology.

7

Service Supply Chains

1. Motivation

The Economist defines services as "anything sold in the trade that cannot be dropped on your foot." According to Levitt,[1] products can be seen as the physical embodiment of the services they deliver. In fact, as shown in Figure 7.1, a growing proportion of the active population in developed economies would describe their jobs as a service operation. Yet with a few exceptions, this book has largely focused on supply chains producing and delivering physical goods to final customers. The question that must be addressed is what portion of the concepts and ideas developed thus far also apply to service settings.

In answering this question, instead of trying to produce a concise definition of services, it would be more useful to focus on the differences between manufacturing and service operations. Following Teboul's[2] classification, these characteristics are summarized in Table 7.1.

There are indeed some key differences between a manufactured product and a service offer. The existence of a tangible product in the former case makes it possible to control the production process and the resulting inventories efficiently. Zero defects are possible as long as the quality management system intercepts nonconforming products and reworks them. Given the nontangible nature of services, effective management of capacity is crucial. The presence of the customer and, in most cases, the active participation of the customer in the service delivery process (the coproduction) renders the traditional inspect-and-correct quality control approach infeasible.

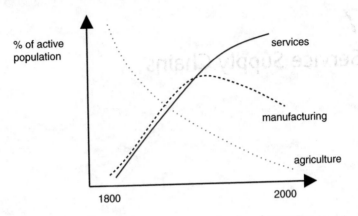

Figure 7.1 Evolution of different sectors in a developed economy.

Table 7.1 Product and service characteristics

Pure Products	**Pure Services**
Transformation	**Performance**
• Tangible goods	• Intangible value
• Inventory management	• Capacity management
• Zero defects; rework	• Zero defections; robustness
Absence of Customer	**Presence of Customer**
• Standardization	• Coproduction
• Centralization of production	• High variability
• Centralization of distribution	• Close locations to customer
• Economies of scale	• Economies of scope
Marketing a Product	**Marketing a Performance**
• Transactional marketing	• Relationship marketing
• Control of channels	• Internal marketing
• Channel efficiencies	• Channel agility

Robust design that is capable of satisfying the requirements of a diverse customer base is necessary to ensure zero defections.

Similarly, while the location of a manufacturing facility or a distribution center is of little interest to the customer of a manufactured product, a convenient location with easy access is an important prerequisite for any effective service system. On the other hand, internal marketing of the service concept to a company's employees, who are the key interface with the customer, is a unique feature of services.

We have to immediately acknowledge that the differences between manufactured products and service offerings are not as clear-cut as listed above, even for pure products (e.g., industrial gases) and pure services (e.g., a session with your personal psychiatrist). Can one classify a *McDonald's* restaurant as a service? Not if you look at the assembly lines found in the kitchen. Is *Peugeot-Citroën* simply a car manufacturer? Not if you consider the dealerships and the after-sales service. In other words, in any activity, there exists a production aspect (or a back office) as well as a service aspect (or a front office). As Teboul puts it, "we are all in services – *more or less*," depending on the relative size of the front and back office, respectively. There exist useful frameworks to understand the dynamics of these two stages, the front and back offices.

The *product-process matrix*[3] that contrasts product characteristics with the capabilities of different production processes provides a convenient model to capture the challenges in the back office. The rows of this matrix show the full spectrum of production processes ranging from a project environment with a unique output to continuous flow with a narrow scope. The columns of the matrix capture some of the key product characteristics, ranging from low-volume high-variety to high-volume low-variety (highly standardized) products. As illustrated with a medical example in Figure 7.2, Hayes and Wheelwright postulate that it makes economic sense to operate in

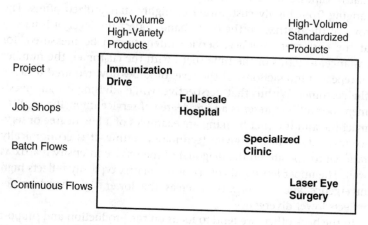

Figure 7.2 The product-process matrix.

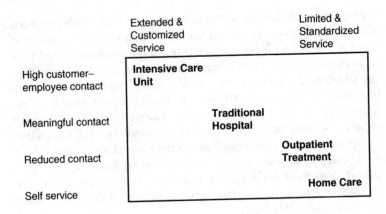

Figure 7.3　Service intensity matrix.

the diagonal of this matrix. Over the years, technological advances such as Flexible Manufacturing Systems attempted to break away from the diagonal by enabling higher levels of flexibility (hence, product variety and/or volume) without increasing the variable production costs.

In a similar spirit, Teboul proposes the *service intensity matrix*, illustrated in Figure 7.3, to capture the challenges in the front office. As in the product–process matrix, the columns of the service intensity matrix capture some of the key characteristics of the service offer, ranging from highly customized to highly standardized offers. The rows of the matrix, on the other hand, reflect the level of intensity at the customer interface. Service intensity can be measured, for instance, in terms of the time spent with the customer, the number of repeated interactions, or the level of know-how required to serve the customer. Within that perspective, while advising on an investment portfolio represents a high degree of service intensity, an ATM machine and Internet banking are examples of a low degree of service intensity. Within a given technology setting, it is economically rational to operate on the diagonal of the service intensity matrix as well. The upper left-hand corner of the matrix typically reflects high divergence and complexity whereas the lower right-hand corner reflects lower divergence.

In the back office, we tend to focus on the production and support aspect of the operations, emphasizing the economies of scale. In the front office, however, we focus on the performance and customer interaction, emphasizing the economies of scope. These differences in focus may lead to difficulties in effectively interfacing the front office with the back office. This challenge is addressed in the next section.

2. Interfacing the front office with the back office

Consider a queueing system where customers arrive at random and seek service from a server. Examples of such systems include barber shops, emergency rooms, and telecommunication systems. Given the different service requirements of each customer, the service times are not constant. One performance measure of interest is the average time customers spend in the system, typically referred to as the cycle time (or flow time) in manufacturing and waiting time in queueing theory. Without drowning in the mathematical details, let us use the following approximation for waiting time:[4]

$$W_q = \left(\frac{CV_a^2 + CV_s^2}{2} \right) \left(\frac{u}{1-u} \right) t_s, \qquad (7.1)$$

where CV_a and CV_s denote the coefficients of variation (σ/μ) for the arrival process and the service process, respectively, which indicates the volatility in these processes. While it may be difficult to estimate the value of CV, a rough assessment of its magnitude may be possible from the physical context. For instance, a CV_a of 1 reveals total randomness in the arrival process; i.e., the observation of a customer arrival provides us with no additional information on the arrival time of the next customer. A large CV_a indicates positively correlated arrivals; i.e., observing one arrival makes further arrivals more likely (e.g., a viral outbreak). Conversely, a negative CV_a indicates negative correlation; i.e., observing one arrival makes further arrivals less likely (e.g., a breakdown in a finite pool of machines). u denotes the utilization rate of the server; ranging from 0 to 1.0, it indicates the load on the server, a proxy for system capacity. Finally, t_s is the average service time.

This intuitive approximation describes the three key drivers of the waiting time, one of the key components of customer experience in the front office. The first one, the average service time, t_s, is the *scale* effect. Intuitively, with short service times, customers spend less time in the system. The second key driver is the utilization rate of the server. The expression $(u/1-u)$ implies that a high utilization of the server (i.e., a heavy load) would drastically increase the average waiting time for the customers. In fact, waiting time increases *exponentially fast* as the utilization rate nears 100%. The last driver of the waiting time is the volatility in the arrival and service processes. A higher level of variance results in higher waiting times.

Further, note the compounding effect these drivers have on the waiting time. A high level of volatility together with high utilization of the server and long service times would make the average waiting times unbearably longer. For example, in an emergency room, there is virtually no control over the arrival pattern of patients; controlling the input volatility is thus impossible. Similarly, as a patient who just suffered a heart attack has drastically different service requirements than a nine-year old with a broken arm, service time volatility is equally high. Hence, in this environment, no matter how expensive of a resource they represent, you cannot insist on a 100% utilization of your physicians without risking an unbearably long waiting time for the emergency patients.

These three drivers can also be viewed as three levers for defining an adequate service experience for the customer through a better interface between the back office and the front office through better product, process, and supply chain design. Specific initiatives can be undertaken to control the volatility in the arrival and service processes and to carefully monitor the utilization rate of the server. Illustrative examples are discussed next.

2.1 Shouldice Hospital

Consider the *Shouldice Hospital*,[5] "a center of excellence for the repair of abdominal wall hernias." Founded in 1945 in the outskirts of Toronto by Dr Earl Shouldice, who developed an innovative surgical procedure enabling rapid recovery, the hospital has thus far hosted over 300,000 patients with over 99% success rate (i.e., no recurrence). The "Shouldice technique," however, is only one aspect of the patient experience. As illustrated by the "Shouldice Pictorial" on the hospital's web site, the campus looks more like a country club than a hospital.

Patients, who had previously filled out a diagnostic survey and taken an appointment for surgery, arrive at the facility in the afternoon to go through an initial screening by one of the surgeons. The objective is to conduct the necessary tests to ensure that the patient indeed requires an intervention and, more importantly, that he/she is physically ready for it. The remainder of the afternoon is dedicated to settling into a semiprivate room, debriefing with a staff nurse about the pre- and postsurgery practices, and socializing with fellow patients. The following morning, the surgery takes place under a local anaesthetic, which enables the patient not only to get up from the operating table and walk to a wheelchair, but also to get moving a few hours after the surgery, playing mini-golf, shooting pool, or doing "aerobics." The patient is usually discharged the following morning.

At *Shouldice*, the front office has a very high degree of service intensity through high levels of interaction with the staff and fellow patients as well as through the special design of the facilities. On the other hand, the back office is run very efficiently. Expression (7.1) holds the key to this seamless interfacing of the front and back offices: *Shouldice* is a *focused factory*! Unlike a general hospital, *Shouldice* does only one thing: repairing abdominal wall hernias. The Shouldice technique requires 90 minutes for the operation (t_s). In addition, by tightly controlling the intake of patients, including a careful screening of their requirements and their physical condition, the unexpected bad surprises are minimized – or even eliminated – virtually reducing all the variability in the service process (CV_s^2). Similarly, there is no variability in the arrival process ($CV_a^2 \approx 0$) as potential patients not only take a self-diagnostic survey but also take appointments for the surgery at the hospital. In such a stable environment, the hospital can afford to achieve a high utilization level for the surgeons and the operating theatres – hence, achieving economies of scale in the back office – without compromising the customer service – i.e., the patient experience – in the front office. This is indeed achieved through a careful design of the product (the service concept) and the process (the Shouldice technique).

2.2 *CIBA Vision* in Europe

While half of the world population requires some type of vision correction, only a small fraction wears contact lenses (5% in the European Union, 9% in Japan, and 19% in the USA). This low penetration among end consumers is mainly driven by the high cost and care requirements for contact lenses, the cumbersome fitting process, and the long-term safety concerns due to low oxygen permeability. Significant improvements in materials as well as in manufacturing technologies, however, are changing this industry drastically. The continuous improvement in materials has enhanced oxygen permeability, enabling the introduction of extended-wear contact lenses. On the manufacturing side, the development of the wet molding (*Lightstream*) technology not only slashed manufacturing costs, making disposable (daily wear) lenses economically viable, but also reduced the manufacturing cycle time from 3 days to 15 seconds! In short, materials and process technology has transformed the contact lens industry (the back office) from a high-cost low-volume industry into a high-volume low-cost one.

This transformation could not leave the downstream channel (the front office) unchanged, particularly blurring the line between the customer and the consumer. Traditionally, the eye care specialist was *CIBA Vision*'s customer. That is, each national sale subsidiary has a close relationship with the ophthalmologist, optometrist, or the fitting studio, providing them with trial sets, taking their orders, and ensuring order fulfilment. The consumer, the contact lens wearer, would only interface with the eye care specialist, typically unaware of the contact lens manufacturer. With the daily-wear disposable lenses, however, the consumer, with the prescription on hand, could visit any one of the optometrist chain outlets – or even the Internet – to order and receive a branded pack of contact lenses. In certain countries, the lenses would be replenished automatically at the consumer's residence.

With these changes in the industry, *CIBA Vision* was considering the centralization of its logistics operations in Europe. The main concern in this significant back office reorganization was how well the back office would be able to support the front office, namely, the diverging business requirements from each channel (ophthalmologists, opticians, eye care chains) in each European country. In particular, the following concerns must be addressed:

Front office

- Local regulations (language, labelling, etc.) as contact lenses are considered to be medical devices.
- Local terms of the trade (payment terms, targets, compensation plans, etc.): while average receivables are 18 days in Denmark, they are approximately 90 days in Italy.

- Local channel characteristics (market penetration, local competition, CRM): while it is necessary to obtain a prescription from an ophthalmologist in France, fitting studios are popular in Scandinavia.
- Revenue recognition (and other financial implications).
- Demand characteristics (average sales, sales volatility, forecasting practices): the average number of shipments is around 1300 in Germany, whereas it hovers around 500 in France with the corresponding inventory levels at 60 days of stock (DOS) and 90 DOS, respectively.
- Service characteristics (order fulfilment process, performance): 8000 SKUs are carried in Germany while only 1500 stock keeping units (SKUs) are held in Scandinavia.
- Costs (WCR, obsolescence, warehousing, headcount, etc.): obsolescence is around 9% of sales in Italy and 5% in the UK.

Back office

- Materials management policies: 15 DOS for A items, 30 DOS for B items, and 120 DOS for C items.
- Production planning and scheduling: given the rapidly growing worldwide demand, the production facilities were running almost at capacity.
- Pick and pack process: with a two-hour picking cycle, a capability to pick 30,000 orders per day that would achieve a 99.9% on time in full (OTIF) service level was targeted.
- Shipping modes for different destinations.
- Quantification of the pooling economies: the safety stock that used to be held in local subsidiaries was centralized, hence reduced.
- *Lightstream* process technology enabling frequent replenishment systems through a 15-second cycle time.

The key challenge in the front office is to push the standardization of customer service without compromising the varying degrees of customer intimacy required in each channel and in each country. The key challenge in the back office is to quantify the magnitude of the cost savings due to pooling economies, the increase in shipping costs, the materials management practices, and ultimately the interface with the production process. The interface challenge between the front office and the back office is illustrated in Figure 7.4.

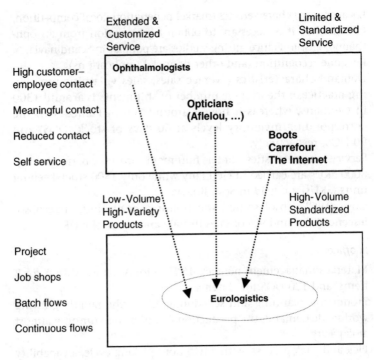

Figure 7.4 Interfacing the front office and the back office for *CIBA Vision*.

The deployed solution, *Eurologistics*, separated three key flows of information, material, and cash to achieve compatibility between the highly diverse front office and the highly standardized back office. As before, the customer is fitted with contact lenses at an eye care professional. The professional would then call the local sales subsidiary to place an order for the lenses. Such orders would typically be placed over the phone. For example, in France, *CIBA Vision*'s sales organization operates a call center in Toulouse that takes telephone orders from the eye care professionals. These orders are immediately transferred through EDI to the *Eurologistics* center in Grosswallstadt. If the requested lenses are in stock, a pick and pack (P&P) order would be printed. With the single P&P sheet, the lenses are picked, packed, and shipped directly to the eye care professional that had originally placed

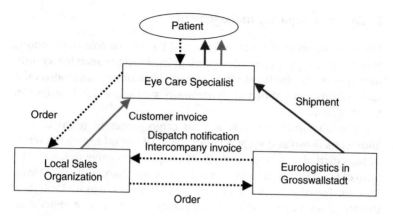

Figure 7.5 The *Eurologistics* solution.

the order with the local sales subsidiary. Simultaneously, a dispatch notification is sent to the local sales subsidiary enabling them to invoice the eye care professional.

As summarized in Figure 7.5, Grosswallstadt operates as a toll distribution center that simply matches orders with inventory and ships them to the requested address. It does not hold any customer database; it does not manage any financial transactions, which remain the responsibility of the local sales subsidiary. Such an approach not only preserves the close relationship that exist in each country between the representatives of the sales subsidiary and the pool of eye care specialists they serve (front office performance) while affording pooling economies for inventory and scale economies for the warehousing and distribution operations (back office efficiency).

Recalling expression (7.1) for the waiting time in a queueing system, we observe that *CIBA Vision* has deployed all three drivers. The streamlining of the P&P process not only reduced the service time to two hours, but the process design virtually eliminated the variability (hence, the coefficient of variation) of the P&P service. Through the dynamic scheduling of its workforce, *CIBA Vision* carefully controls the utilization rate of the server. Finally, the pooling of the demand from all the countries across Europe reduces the coefficient of variation of the order arrival process through pooling.

3. Dynamic capacity management

The two examples in Section 2 showed the crucial role the product, process, and supply chain design plays in achieving seamless coordination between the front office and the back office. There also exist tactical initiatives aimed at dynamically managing this interface in the short run.

Lufthansa Cargo[6] is the largest air cargo carrier in terms of ton-kilometers flown and second largest (behind *Federal Express*) in terms of tons carried. Air cargo business is a capital-intensive industry; the ratio of tangible assets to sales was 14% for the German retailer *Metro*, 26% for *DaimlerChrysler*, and 60% for *Lufthansa Cargo* in 2000. It is therefore no surprise that management of capacity, a perishable good, is of crucial importance.

Revenue Management (RM) has received considerable attention in recent years. RM, which exploits the differences in the marginal WTP among customers, attempts to find a balance between the fact that unused capacity is lost forever, and that higher margin demand arrives at the last minute. Most passenger airline companies are successfully using RM practices. There are, however, complicating factors in air cargo such as multi-dimensional unit loads (e.g., weight, volume, etc.), stacking loss due to the shape and position of the cargo, and one-way, unbalanced flows. Moreover, 90–95% of the volume is controlled by freight forwarders, rendering direct customer contact virtually impossible.

In this set-up, the challenge for *Lufthansa Cargo* is to determine the optimal space allocation to various cargo classes to maximize fill rate and expected revenue. For example, as illustrated in Figure 7.6, how much space should be reserved for express cargo that commands higher prices and how much to sell *en bloc* in advance?

One approach to the capacity management challenge is to dynamically price available capacity to reflect the demand-supply conditions, which may irritate potential customers. Another approach is to secure a certain level of load (utilization) through long-term firm-commitment contracts and put the remaining capacity on the spot market. Capacity options can then be used as a mechanism to hedge against spot-market volatility (also giving *Lufthansa Cargo* additional information to forecast potential demand with higher accuracy). A capacity option represents the right – but not the obligation – for the

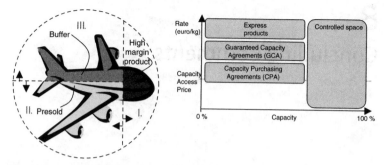

Figure 7.6 Managing capacity at *Lufthansa* (Hellerman and Huchzermeier, 2002).

freight forwarder to purchase cargo capacity at a predetermined price. The option buyer, the forwarder, will exercise the option only if the spot price is higher than the exercise price of the option. The system is, therefore, "Pareto-improving" for the shipper (lower rates), for the freight forwarder (higher service levels), and the carrier (more accurate demand forecasts and higher fill rates).

4. Summary

- While product supply chains focus on economies of scale and efficiency through materials management, service supply chains focus on economies of scope and effectiveness through capacity management.
- Given that most value propositions consist of a product and service bundle, the product-focused back office must be interfaced with the customer-focused front office in spite of the divergent priorities.
- In the long run, an intelligent design of products, processes, and supply chains facilitates this coordination. In the short run, revenue management is a dynamic way of managing capacity as a perishable good.

8
Concluding Comments

In this book, we have emphasized three key messages:

- **Value:** While the traditional approaches to SCM have favored cost minimization, we believe that SCM is a value enabler with strategic decisions in supply chain design leading to value creation and tactical decisions in supply chain coordination leading to value capture.
- **Alignment:** In the absence of a vertically integrated industry structure with clear command and control lines, it is difficult to coordinate the players in an ecosystem with divergent and typically conflicting interests. While trust-based collaborative practices are the ultimate goal, adequate economic incentives should be designed to ensure the much-needed alignment.
- **Sustainability:** Just like products and processes, supply chain solutions have a limited shelf life. As a consequence, supply chain design should be viewed as a dynamic process, as the capability to design and assemble assets, organizations, skill sets, and competencies for a *series* of competitive advantages, rather than a set of activities held together by low transaction costs.

Such a focus was the result of various key initiatives undertaken over the past few decades to manage the key interfaces in a more effective fashion. As illustrated in Figure 8.1, JIT has been the sweeping philosophy in the 1980s with the aim of promoting mutually beneficial relationships between a manufacturer and its supply base. The ECR movement, which was introduced in the 1990s, aimed at

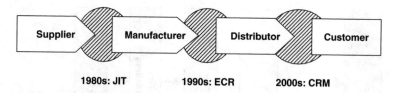

Figure 8.1 Major initiatives along the supply chain.

creating transparent relationships within the downstream channel. With the key advances in the information technology, CRM was introduced to put the customer in the driver's seat of the ecosystem. With this background, the alignment of all the players in the ecosystem must be the top priority of all supply chain professionals to make modern supply chains an enabler for value creation and a source of a sustainable competitive advantage.

We have started this book by defining the supply chain as a platform deployed to manage three key flows: material, information, and cash. We finish this book with an example that illustrates how that platform could be designed so that these flows do not all have to go through the same channels.

HP Business Desktop Division (BDD)

In the third quarter of 2006, *HP* has recaptured the top position of worldwide PC shipments from *Dell*. Even a few months prior to this reversal, matching *Dell* was thought to be very difficult, if not impossible. Analysts were stating that no matter how deeply *HP* could cut costs, it would never be able to build a zero-cost channel to compete with *Dell*, which did not have such costs due to its direct model. In fact, the Business Desktop supply chain in the mid-1990s, which is depicted in Figure 8.2, shows the magnitude of the challenge.[1] The ecosystem consisted of worldwide suppliers, assembly facilities, tier-1 distributors, and tier-2 value-added resellers (VAR). Inventory levels at various stages are also shown in the figure. The fact that 1% is shaved off of the selling price of a PC every week is sufficient to illustrate the severity of the challenge.

HP's supply chain redesign efforts started with the realization that the hardware-related costs represent about 25% of the total cost of ownership for a PC. This, in turn, has reoriented the organization

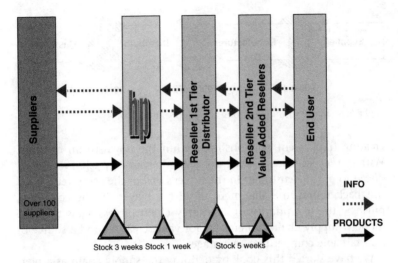

Figure 8.2   *HP*'s BDD supply chain in mid-1990s.

from selling boxes to providing business computing solutions. The customer-facing front office has thus been redefined as depicted in Figure 8.3. At one end of the spectrum, "platform buyers" looked for hardware only where their in-house IT capability took care of the installation, training, and maintenance.

On the other end of the spectrum, the "solutions buyer" relied on systems vendor for the total solution. For a high-touch relationship, *HP* decoupled the information and material flows as depicted in Figure 8.4.

In terms of the information flows, *HP* placed itself right in front of the customer ahead of the distributors and VARs. Such a positioning enabled *HP* to obtain timely and undistorted market information. Then, *HP* adopted the role of an orchestrator along the supply chain. For platform buyers, *HP* triggered the production of the hardware, which would subsequently be delivered to the customer by the distributor. For the solutions buyers, *HP* started by designing a solution and triggered the production of the hardware component of that solution. The solution would then be deployed by the VAR at the customer site as a product and service bundle. As for the financial flows, each partner in the system was remunerated in a fashion that is commensurate to the value they have delivered to the final customer.

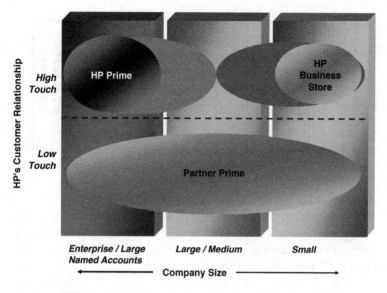

Figure 8.3 HP's customer orientation.

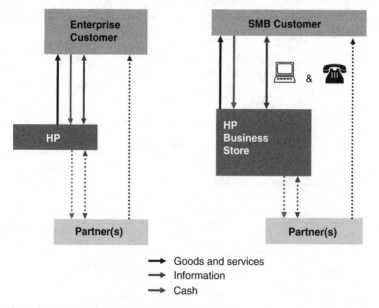

Figure 8.4 Material, information, and cash flows.

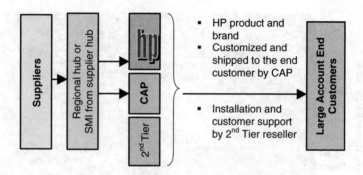

Figure 8.5   The new *HP* supply chain.

To enable such a business model, HP has drastically reorganized the upstream supply chain through such initiatives as the creation of supplier hubs, outsourcing of assembly facilities, and channel assembly. This is depicted in Figure 8.5.

Today, *HP* pursues "advanced local customization" in fast-growing markets (for example, the Middle East) by local assembly of PCs in Saudi Arabia, where bulky boxes are directly shipped through sea lanes from China and small but expensive critical parts are air freighted from eastern Europe.

Appendix: Standard Normal Distribution and Standard Loss Function

z	F(z)	L(z)	z	F(z)	L(z)
−4.0	0.0000	4.0000	−0.6	0.2743	0.7687
−3.9	0.0000	3.9000	−0.5	0.3085	0.6978
−3.8	0.0001	3.8000	−0.4	0.3446	0.6304
−3.7	0.0001	3.7000	−0.3	0.3821	0.5668
−3.6	0.0002	3.6000	−0.2	0.4207	0.5069
−3.5	0.0002	3.5001	−0.1	0.4602	0.4509
−3.4	0.0003	3.4001	0.0	0.5000	0.3989
−3.3	0.0005	3.3001	0.1	0.5398	0.3509
−3.2	0.0007	3.2002	0.2	0.5793	0.3069
−3.1	0.0010	3.1003	0.3	0.6179	0.2668
−3.0	0.0013	3.0004	0.4	0.6554	0.2304
−2.9	0.0019	2.9005	0.5	0.6915	0.1978
−2.8	0.0026	2.8008	0.6	0.7257	0.1687
−2.7	0.0035	2.7011	0.7	0.7580	0.1429
−2.6	0.0047	2.6015	0.8	0.7881	0.1202
−2.5	0.0062	2.5020	0.9	0.8159	0.1004
−2.4	0.0082	2.4027	1.0	0.8413	0.0833
−2.3	0.0107	2.3037	1.1	0.8643	0.0686
−2.2	0.0139	2.2049	1.2	0.8849	0.0561
−2.1	0.0179	2.1065	1.3	0.9032	0.0455
−2.0	0.0228	2.0085	1.4	0.9192	0.0367
−1.9	0.0287	1.9111	1.5	0.9332	0.0293
−1.8	0.0359	1.8143	1.6	0.9452	0.0232
−1.7	0.0446	1.7183	1.7	0.9554	0.0183
−1.6	0.0548	1.6232	1.8	0.9641	0.0143
−1.5	0.0668	1.5293	1.9	0.9713	0.0111
−1.4	0.0808	1.4367	2.0	0.9772	0.0085
−1.3	0.0968	1.3455	2.1	0.9821	0.0065
−1.2	0.1151	1.2561	2.2	0.9861	0.0049
−1.1	0.1357	1.1686	2.3	0.9893	0.0037
−1.0	0.1587	1.0833	2.4	0.9918	0.0027
−0.9	0.1841	1.0004	2.5	0.9938	0.0020
−0.8	0.2119	0.9202	2.6	0.9953	0.0015
−0.7	0.2420	0.8429	2.7	0.9965	0.0011

(Continued)

(*Continued*)

z	F(z)	L(z)	z	F(z)	L(z)
2.8	0.9974	0.0008	3.5	0.9998	0.0001
2.9	0.9981	0.0005	3.6	0.9998	0.0000
3.0	0.9987	0.0004	3.7	0.9999	0.0000
3.1	0.9990	0.0003	3.8	0.9999	0.0000
3.2	0.9993	0.0002	3.9	1.0000	0.0000
3.3	0.9995	0.0001	4.0	1.0000	0.0000
3.4	0.9997	0.0001			

Notes

Preface

1. Kurt Salmon and Associates, 1993, *Efficient Consumer Response: Enhancing Consumer Value in the Grocery Industry.*

Chapter 1

1. *L'Usine Nouvelle*, October 1998.
2. M.E. Porter, 1980, *Competitive Strategy: Techniques for Analyzing Industries and Competitors.*
3. The WEEE (Waste Electrical and Electronic Equipment) Directive within the European Union defines the boundaries of responsibility within the electronics industry.
4. An excellent synthesis of this research can be found in *Factory Physics* (2001) by W.J. Hopp and M.L. Spearman.
5. A.P. McAfee and M. Ashia, 2001, *Synchra Systems.*
6. C.H. Fine, 1998, *Clockspeed: Winning Industry Control in the Age of Temporary Advantage.*

Chapter 2

1. C.H. Fine, 1998, *Clockspeed: Winning Industry Control in the Age of Temporary Advantage.*
2. S.D. Young and S.F. O'Byrne, 2001, *EVA and Value-Based Management.*
3. *International Herald Tribune*, 16 June 2006.
4. *International Herald Tribune*, 3 July 2006.
5. K. Hendricks and V. Singhal, 2003, The Effect of Supply Chain Glitches on Shareholder Value.

Chapter 3

1. S. Dutta and E. Yücesan, 1996, *Rank Xerox France: The Logistics Process.*
2. A.S. Grove, 1999, *Only the Paranoid Survive: How to Exploit the Crisis Points that Challenge Every Company.* Doubleday, New York, NY.
3. C.H. Fine, 1998, *Clockspeed: Winning Industry Control in the Age of Temporary Advantage.*
4. H. Mendelson and R.R. Pillai, 1999, Industry Clockspeed: Measurement and Operational Implications.
5. T. Randall, 1998, Managing Product Variety: A Study of the Bicycle Industry.
6. M.L. Fisher, 1997, What is the Right Supply Chain for Your Product?

7. *Business Week,* Why the Supply Chain Broke Down? March 19, 2001, p. 39.
8. S. Ülkü, B.L. Toktay, and E. Yücesan, 2006, Risk Ownership in Contract Manufacturing.
9. S. Ülkü, B.L. Toktay, and E. Yücesan, 2005, The Impact of Outsourced Manufacturing on Timing of Entry in Uncertain Markets.
10. C.H. Fine, 1998, *Clockspeed.*
11. C.H. Fine, 1998, *Clockspeed.*
12. R. Adner, 2006, Match your Innovation Strategy to Your Innovation Ecosystem.
13. D.B. Yoffie and M. Kwak, 2006, With Friends Like These.

Chapter 4

1. The newsvendor framework is discussed in Chapter 5.
2. L. Kopczak and H. Lee, 1994, HP Deskjet Printer Supply Chain (A).
3. J.D.C. Little, 1992, Tautologies, Models, and Theories: Can We Find "Laws" of Manufacturing.
4. R.H. Wilson, 1934, A Scientific Routine for Stock Control.

Chapter 5

1. H. Lee, P. Padmanabhan, and S. Whang, 1997, The Paralyzing Curse of the Bullwhip Effect in the Supply Chain.
2. J. Hammond, 1994, *Barilla SpA (A),* HBS Case Study.
3. CPFR.org.
4. The Straights Times, *Santa Emma,* 6 November 2006.
5. G.P. Cachon and M.A. Lariviere, 2001, Turning Supply Chains into Revenue Chains.

Chapter 6

1. D.A. Garvin, 1987, *DEC: The End Point Model,* HBS Case Study.

Chapter 7

1. T. Levitt, 1972, Production Line Approach to Service.
2. J. Teboul, 2006, *Service is Front Stage: Positioning Services for Value Advantage.*
3. R. Hayes and S. Wheelwright, 1984, *Restoring Our Competitive Edge: Competing through Manufacturing.*
4. J.F.C. Kingman, 1961, The Single Server Queue in Heavy Traffic.
5. www.shouldice.com.
6. R. Hellerman and A. Huchzermeier, 2002, *Lufthansa Cargo AG.*

Chapter 8

1. L.N. Van Wassenhove, J. Teboul and E. Yücesan, 2004, *Supply Chain Evolution at HP,* INSEAD Case Study.

References

Adner, R. 2006. Match Your Innovation Strategy to Your Innovation Ecosystem. *Harvard Business Review*, April, 98–107.

Akkermans, H.A., P. Bogerd, E. Yücesan, and L.V. Wassenhove. 2003. The Impact of ERP on Supply Chain Management: Exploratory Findings from a European Delphi Study. *European Journal of Operational Research*, 146, 284–301.

Amit, R. and C. Zott. 2001. Value Creation in e-Business. *Strategic Management Journal*, 22, 493–520.

Bailey, J.P. and J.Y. Bakos. 1997. An Exploratory Study of the Emerging Role of the Electronic Intermediaries. *International Journal of Electronic Commerce*, 1, 7–20.

Cachon, G.P. and M.A. Lariviere. 2001. Turning Supply Chains into Revenue Chains. *Harvard Business Review*, 3, 20–21.

Dutta, S. and E. Yücesan. 1996. *Rank Xerox France: The Logistics Process*, INSEAD.

Dyer, J.H. and K. Nobeoka. 2000. Creating and Managing a High-Performance Knowledge-Sharing Network: the Toyota Case. *Strategic Management Journal*, 21.3, 345–367.

Evans, P. and T.S. Wurster. 1999. *Blown to Bits: How the New Economics of Information Transforms Strategy*. Harvard Business School Press, Boston, MA.

Evans, P. and T.S. Wurster. 2000. *Blown to Bits*. HBS Press.

Fine, C.H. 1998. *Clockspeed: Winning Industry Control in the Age of Temporary Advantage*, Perseus Books.

Fisher, M.L. 1997. What is the Right Supply Chain for Your Products? *Harvard Business Review*, March–April, 105–116.

Garvin, D.A. 1997. DEC: The EndPoint Model (A), Harvard Business School Case 9-688-059.

Gulati, R., N. Nohria, and A. Zaheer. 2000. Strategic Networks. *Strategic Management Journal*, 21.3, 203–215.

Hammond, J. 1994. Barilla SpA (A). Harvard Business School.

Hayes, R. and S. Wheelwright. 1984. *Restoring Our Competitive Edge: Competing through Manufacturing*. Wiley.

Hellerman, R. and A. Huchzermeier. 2002. *Lufthansa Cargo AG*, WHU, Koblenz.

Hendricks, K. and V. Singhal. 2003. The Effect of Supply Chain Glitches on Shareholder Value. *Journal of Operations Management*, 21, 501–522.

Hopp, W.J. and M.L. Spearman. 2001. *Factory Physics: Foundations of Manufacturing Management*, 2nd Edition, McGraw-Hill, NY.

Kaplan, S. and M. Shawney. 2000. E-Hbs: the New B2B Marketplaces. *Harvard Business Review*, May–June, 97–103.

Kingman, J.F.C. 1961. The Single Server Queue in Heavy Traffic. *Proceedings of the Cambridge Philosophical Society*, 57, 902–904.

Kopczak, L. and H. Lee. 1994. HP Deskjet Printer Supply Chain (A). Case Study. Graduate School of Business, Stanford University.

Kurt Salmon and Associates. 1993. Efficient Consumer Response: Enhancing Consumer Value in the Grocery Industry. Report. Kurt salmon and Associates.

Lee, H., P. Padmanabhan, and S. Whang. 1997. The Paralyzing Curse of the Bullwhip Effect in the Supply Chain. *Sloan Management Review*, Spring 1997, 93–102.

Levitt, T. 1972. Production Line Approach to Service. *Harvard Business Review*, 50.5, 41–52.

Little, J.D.C. 1992. Tautologies, Models, and Theories: Can We Find "Laws" of Manufacturing, *IIE Transactions*, 24, 7–13.

Malone, T.W., J. Yates, and R.I. Benjamin. 1987. Electronic Markets and Electronic Hierarchies, *Communications of the ACM*, 30, 484–497.

McAfee, R.P. and J. MicMillan. 1987. Auctions and Bidding. *Journal of Economic Literature*, 25.2, 699–738.

McAfee, A.P. and M. Ashia. 2001. *Synchra Systems*, Harvard Business School.

Mendelson, H. and R.R. Pillai. 1999. Industry Clockspeed: Measurement and Operational Implications. *Manufacturing and Service Operations Management*, 1, 1–20.

Moitra, D. and J. Ganesh. 2005. Web Services and Flexible Business Process: Towards the Adaptive Enterprise. *Information and Management*, 42, 921–933.

Palmer, J.W. and M.L. Markus. 2000. The Performance Impacts of Quick Response and Strategic Alignment in Specialty Retailing. *Information Systems Research*, 11.3, 241–259.

Porter. M.E. 1980. *Competitive Strategy: Techniques for Analyzing Industries and Competitors*. The Free Press.

Randall, T., K. Ulrich, M. Fisher, and D. Reibstein. 1998. Managing Product Variety: a Study of the Bicycle Industry. In: *Managing Product Variety*, Teck Ho and Christ Tang (eds). Kluwer Academic Publishers, 177–206.

Sodhi, M.S. 2001. Applications and Opportunities for Operations Research in Internet-Enabled Supply Chains and Electronic Markets. *Interfaces*, 31.2, 56–69.

Stoll, H.W. 1986. Design for Manufacture: an Overview. *Applied Mechanical Review*, 39.9, 236–243.

Swaminathan, J.M. and S.R. Tayur. 2003. Models for Supply Chains in ess-Business. *Management Science*, 49.10, 1387–1406.

Tayur, S., S. Ganeshan, and M. Magazine. 1998. *Quantitative Models for Supply Chain Management*, Kluwer Academic Publishers.

Teboul, J., L.N. Van Wassenhove, and E. Yücesan. 1999. HP.

Teboul, J. 2006. *Service is Front Stage: Positioning Services for Value Advantage*. Palgrave Macmillan.

Tsay, A.A., S. Nahmias, and N. Agrawal. 1999. Modeling Supply Chain Contracts: a Review. In: *Quantitative Models for Supply Chain Management*, Tayur, S., R. Ganeshan, and M. Magazine, (eds). Kluwer Academic Publishers, 299–336.

Young, S.D. and S.F O'Byrne. 2001. *EVA and Value-Based Management*. McGraw-Hill.

Upton, D.M. and A. McAfee. 1996. The Real Virtual Factory. *Harvard Business Review*, July–August, 123–133.

Upton, D.M. and A.P. McAfee. 1997. A Path-Based Approach to Information Technology in Manufacturing. HBS Working Paper 97-094. To appear in *International Journal of Technology Management*.

Ülkü, S., B.L. Toktay, and E. Yücesan. 2006. Risk Ownership in Contract Manufacturing. *Manufacturing and Service Operations Management*, Forthcoming.

Ülkü, S., B.L. Toktay, and E. Yücesan. 2005. The Impact of Outsourced Manufacturing on Timing of Entry in Uncertain Markets. *Production and Operations Management*, 14.3, 301–314.

Van Wassenhove, L.N., J. Teboul and E. Yücesan. 2004. *Supply Chain Evolution at HP*. INSEAD. Case study.

Van Weele, A.J. 2005. *Purchasing and Supply Chain Management: Analysis, Strategy, Planning and Practice*. 4th edn, Thomson.

Wang, C.X. and M. Benaroch. 2004. Supply Chain Coordination in Supplier Centric B2B Electronic Markets. *International Journal of Production Economics*, 92, 113–124.

Wilson, R.H. 1934. A Scientific Routine for Stock Control. *Harvard Business Review*, 13.1, 116–128.

Yoffie, D.B. and M. Kwak. 2006. With Friends Like These. *Harvard Business Review*, September, 89–98.

Index